STEPHEN FRINK

A diver inspects a coral reef in Biscayne National Park.

AMERICA'S HIDDEN TREASURES

Exploring Our Little-Known National Parks

Prepared by the Book Division
National Geographic Society, Washington, D.C.

AMERICA'S HIDDEN TREASURES
Exploring Our Little-Known National Parks

Contributing Authors: Seymour L. Fishbein,
  Kim Heacox, Tom Melham, Cynthia Russ Ramsey,
  Scott Thybony, Jennifer C. Urquhart

Contributing Photographers: Tom Bean,
  Jay Dickman, Stephen Frink, Michael Melford,
  Richard Olsenius, Phil Schofield, James A. Sugar,
  Medford Taylor, Norbert Wu

Published by The National Geographic Society
  Reg Murphy, *President and Chief Executive Officer*
  Gilbert M. Grosvenor, *Chairman of the Board*
  Nina D. Hoffman, *Senior Vice President*

Prepared by The Book Division
  William R. Gray, *Vice President and Director*
  Charles Kogod, *Assistant Director*
  Barbara A. Payne, *Editorial Director*

Staff for this Special Publication
  Mary B. Dickinson, *Managing Editor*
  Thomas B. Powell, III, *Illustrations Editor*
  Suez B. Kehl, *Art Director*
  Patricia F. Frakes, *Senior Researcher*
  Timothy H. Ewing, *Researcher*
  Richard M. Crum, Edward Lanouette,
      Tom Melham, Cynthia Russ Ramsay,
      Scott Thybony, Jennifer C. Urquhart,
      Picture Legend Writers
  Sandra F. Lotterman, *Editorial Assistant*
  Karen Dufort Sligh, *Illustrations Assistant*
  Lewis R. Bassford, *Production Project Manager*
  Heather Guwang, H. Robert Morrison,
      Richard S. Wain, *Production*
  Karen F. Edwards, Elizabeth G. Jevons,
      Artemis S. Lampathakis, Fadi Aziz Melki,
      Teresita Cóquia Sison, Marilyn J. Williams,
      Staff Assistants

Manufacturing and Quality Management
  George V. White, *Director;* John T. Dunn,
      Associate Director; Vincent P. Ryan, *Manager;*
      and R. Gary Colbert

Bryan K. Knedler, *Indexer*

Maps by R.R. Donnelly & Sons Company,
  Cartographic Services, Lancaster, Pennsylvania,
  based on National Park Service sources

Bolt from the blue lends drama to the badlands of North Dakota's Theodore Roosevelt National Park.

PRECEDING PAGES: A quartet of ducks preens for a new day at Voyageurs National Park in Minnesota.

MICHAEL MELFORD (LEFT); RICHARD OLSENIUS (PRECEDING PAGES)

Foreword	8	CHANNEL ISLANDS	92
NORTH CASCADES	10	GUADALUPE MOUNTAINS	118
VOYAGEURS	38	BISCAYNE	146
THEODORE ROOSEVELT	66	KATMAI	170

TOM BEAN

Notes on Contributors,
Acknowledgments, and
Additional Reading   196
Index   197
Parks at a Glance   200

Indulging in an age-old rite, an
Alaskan brown bear angles for a meal of
sockeye salmon at Brooks Falls in Alaska's
Katmai National Park and Preserve.

Foreword

By T. H. Watkins
Editor of Wilderness, *the magazine of The Wilderness Society*

AMERICA'S NATIONAL PARK SYSTEM was the best idea we ever had, in the opinion of James Bryce, former British ambassador to the United States. He was speaking in the early years of this century, when there were in fact not many parks—Yellowstone (the first), Yosemite, Sequoia, Mount Rainier, and a few more. Today, there are 374 National Park units, including numerous historic sites and battlefields, their area totaling more than 83 million acres. Clearly, not only was it one of our best ideas, but also one of our biggest.

But not big enough—not to accommodate everyone everywhere all the time. The parks were established so that Americans could enjoy the beauty, the wildness, and the solitude of some portions of the natural world that had not been overrun by the march of progress. They have served that purpose well, and we are the better for it. But many of the parks are in danger, as the saying goes, of being loved to death. Great Smoky Mountains National Park in Tennessee-North Carolina received more than nine million visits in 1995, Grand Canyon in Arizona more than 4.5 million, and Yosemite in California nearly four million. The parks are still beautiful, still the "crown jewels" of the American landscape. Nevertheless, visitation frequently brings too many of those very things parks were meant to give us relief from—crowds, parking lots, traffic congestion, even smog. All the while, logging, mining, grazing, and real estate development on the edges of many of the parks add their own measure of disturbance.

None of this helps much to create a "wilderness experience," a fact that gives the other, lesser known parks in the system more importance. They are jewels in their own right—islands of natural magnificence that satisfy the deep human yearning to find connection with the life and beauty around us. Many are very little known indeed. Others are fairly hard to get to. All are worth the effort.

This book tells you about seven of these splendidly unrenowned places, selected not merely because they are little known but also because they represent a wide geographic spread and offer a diversity of landscape and experience—from the wondrous desert jumble of mountains and twisting canyons in Guadalupe Mountains National Park to the almost mythic world of wind, water, and forested islands in Voyageurs. Like their better known icons, these and the scores of other unpublicized parks remind us that, while we have not saved all that we should have saved—and not fully protected all that we have—there is still plenty of reason to agree with James Bryce.

Fed by snowmelt, a rivulet tumbles down a rocky slope into Boston Basin in Washington's North Cascades National Park. "Waterfalls are as common as dandelions here," notes a recent visitor.

KENT & DONNA DANNEN

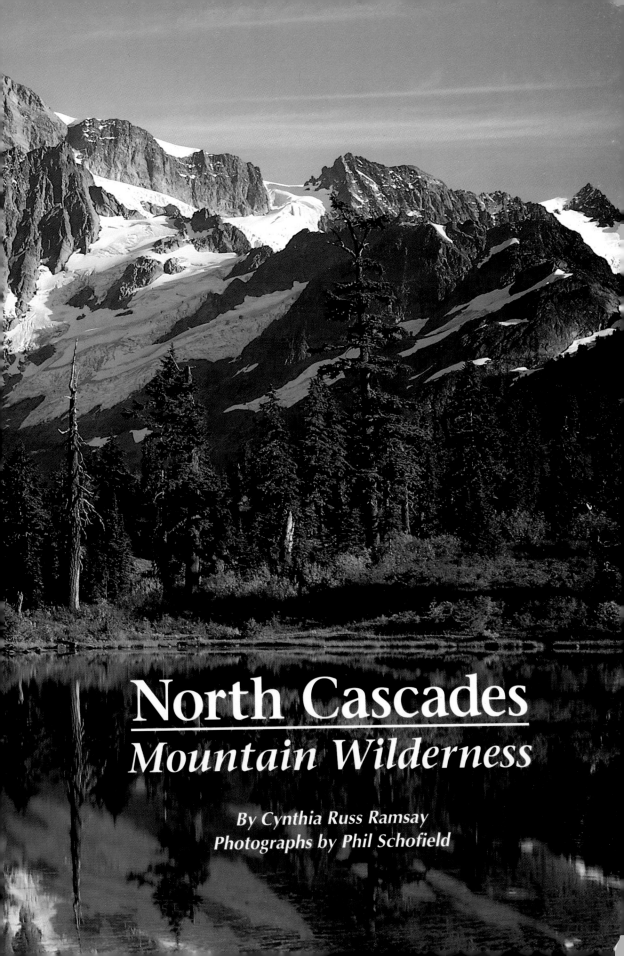

North Cascades
Mountain Wilderness

By Cynthia Russ Ramsay
Photographs by Phil Schofield

*J*AGGED SPIRES and knife-edge ridges cut with sharp precision into the enamel blue sky. Below the rim of mountains a broad sweep of snow and ice shines like molten glass, the dazzling expanse accenting the dark cragginess of the heights. Light breezes coming off the white landscape carry a welcome coolness, but under the hot, high July sun, winter is retreating from Boston Basin—dripping, trickling, splashing exuberantly away in the radiant light.

Silvery cascades surging with snowmelt trellis the cliffs. On the receding snowfield below, meltwater as clear as crystal glazes the surface and seeps downhill. The runoff falls in cataracts where it tumbles over rock outcrops. Rivulets spill into the sodden ground at the snow line, where the green buds of glacier lilies make their debut through the gray-white slush. On the slope just below, the yellow petals have unfolded, bringing a flood of color to the meadow. Scattered patches of heather also proclaim the arrival of spring with their clusters of pink flowers.

This season brings mountaineers with ice axes and climbing ropes who come for the challenges of Forbidden Peak and Mount Torment, which rim Boston Basin. I came for the view and left with the grandeur of North Cascades National Park imprinted on my mind.

It took about four hours on a steep, faint trail to hike up to that resplendent high, wide mountain bowl. Other treks may take days over routes that are acts of courage for even experienced climbers.

You can see some of the classic North Cascades vistas of waterfalls and glacier-draped peaks along Washington State Route 20. The paved road, known as the North Cascades Highway, crosses the 684,244-acre park complex, which was established by Congress in 1968 and includes the Ross Lake and Lake Chelan National Recreation Areas. A

Springtime brings a bright profusion of pink monkey flowers and yellow groundsels to a mountain meadow.

PRECEDING PAGES: Massive ridges and glaciers on Mount Shuksan tower above the dark mirror of Picture Lake in North Cascades National Park, a realm of lush woodlands and rugged mountainscapes.

CHARLES MAUZY (OPPOSITE); GEORGE & MONSERRATE SCHWARTZ / RIC ERGENBRIGHT PHOTOGRAPHY (PRECEDING PAGES)

50-mile ferry ride on Lake Chelan or a floatplane trip to the isolated settlement of Stehekin lets visitors enter the rugged mountain wilderness without fording streams, scrambling through brush, and hauling backpacks up vertical miles. The park offers boating and fishing on lakes, rafting on the Skagit and Stehekin Rivers, and camping at established campgrounds. But to really experience the wild majesty of the North Cascades, you must, as former Park Superintendent John Earnst puts it, walk into that maelstrom of peaks and forests on your own two feet.

The Skagit River penetrates this mountain barrier, but ferocious rapids in the Skagit Gorge once made the upper reaches unnavigable. Today three dams have tamed the Skagit, and the three reservoirs—Ross Lake, Diablo Lake, and Gorge Lake—provide the city of Seattle with much of its electricity. But roads and trails into the mountains remain few, and some are closed by storms and heavy snow for nearly half the year. The maze of mountains and roller coaster timberlands tangled with brush and toppled trees have kept vast sections of the park's backcountry one of the wildest places in North America.

"YOU CAN SPEND A DAY covering just three miles if you are bushwhacking," said Saul Weisberg, a biologist and skilled mountaineer. Saul devotes much of his energy to directing the North Cascades Institute, a nonprofit educational organization offering field seminars for adults and special programs for kids. "Our mission is to help people become aware of the interactions of plants, animals, geology, and weather in this corner of the world."

It was sunny when Saul, photographer Phil Schofield, and I set out from the Thunder Creek trailhead on a four-day trek, but our rain gear was readily accessible in the top of our packs. The Cascades begin only 30 air miles from Puget Sound, and storms and moisture-laden winds sweeping off the Pacific can roll in quickly.

"Monotonous fair weather can't nourish these majestic trees and the masses of ferns and shrubs at their feet, so I've learned to like the gray days when the forest drips and glistens with rain," said Saul as we stepped onto the trail. "And the long winters pile up snow, feeding the glaciers that give these mountains their dramatic shapes."

From time to time thin shafts of sunlight filtered through the canopy, but mostly we walked in cool shade through a colonnade of western hemlocks and western red cedars with fluted trunks. These evergreen giants, rising straight and bare, towered above the leafy maples and alders in the understory. The matted ground was a palette of greens where thickets of low-growing shrubs—huckleberry, salal, thimbleberry, and spiny devil's club with leaves the size of dinner plates—competed for space with lacy ferns and carpets of moss. Even the light seemed green amid this pandemonium of vegetation.

NORTH CASCADES NATIONAL PARK

LOCATION: Washington
ESTABLISHED: October 2, 1968
SIZE: 684,244 acres
Includes Ross Lake and Lake Chelan
National Recreation Areas

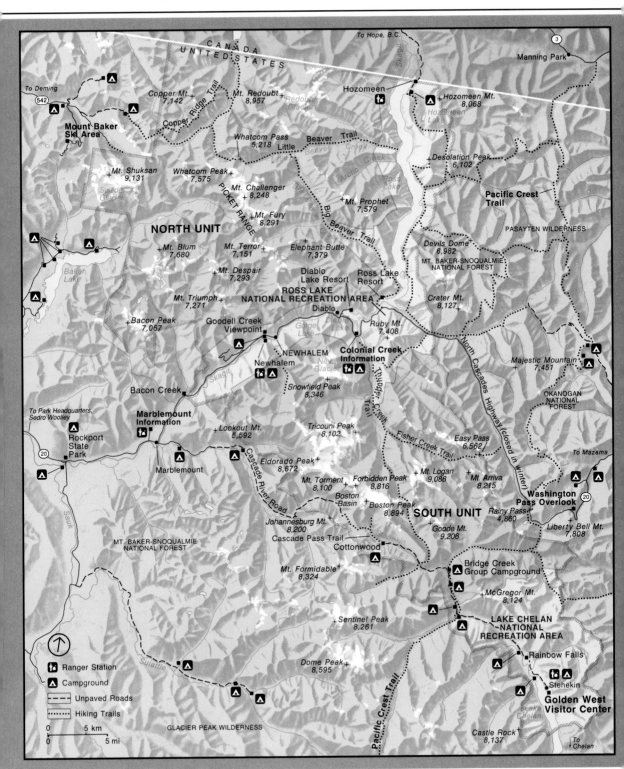

Foamflowers, like specks of froth, and clumps of bunchberry with creamy petal-like bracts banked the path, tempering the green mosaic. Most of the orchids were inconspicuous, but here and there pinedrops sprouted gaudily from the mossy ground like spears of rose red asparagus with tiny flowerets at the tip.

North Cascades vegetation is particularly rich and varied. As many as 1,700 species of vascular plants have been identified. "There are so many different habitats for them to grow in," said Saul.

The spectrum of life starts down in the ancient forests of the lowlands and goes up to the stony rubble of glacial moraines, where fuzzy dwarf plants take root. Precipitation adds another variable, ranging from 110 inches a year on the west side of the mountains to an average of 35 inches in the rain shadow of the Cascade Crest in the east.

I looked forward to lunch, more for the release from my pack than for the chunks of cheese and sticky pieces of dried fruit. A log provided a comfortable place to sit, and the view of Thunder Creek rushing toward Diablo Lake was as soothing as its melody. Flowing from a series of glaciers in the high country, Thunder Creek was opaque with glacial flour—the silt of mountains pulverized to dust.

ON THE SECOND DAY we took the trail that followed Fisher Creek, stopping on the ridge that separates the two streams to gaze at Tricouni Peak, looming above the valley. Snow glistened with hard brilliance from the couloirs and cirques—steep gorges and hollows scoured by past glaciers. Avalanches had also left their marks on the mountain. The timbered slopes were streaked with the emerald hue of alders and maples. Their bright color marked the chutes where snowslides had blasted old-growth evergreens out of the way. Saul explained that alders are successful opportunists, staking their claim fast when they're not stifled by shade. Their seeds are in the ground just waiting for sunlight.

Nothing better illustrates the intense competition for space in these old-growth forests than the spectacle of life springing from the massive trunk of a tree lying on the floor. I never ceased to marvel at the seedlings, saplings, tall trees, mosses, mushrooms, ferns, all sprouting from the slowly crumbling bole of a fallen hemlock or Douglas fir. These "nurse logs" live on for hundreds of years, sustaining plant life and providing food for armies of insects and shelter to many species of birds and small mammals. In their noble decay, the logs conjured for me a perspective of centuries.

From somewhere in the brush a rufous-sided towhee complained about our intrusion, scolding us with a clear, chiming melody. From time to time, other birdsongs drifted down from the canopy— bubbles of sound shimmering above the soft music of Fisher Creek.

The days were pleasant as we dawdled over whatever caught our fancy: a western fence lizard with iridescent scales; a bloblike yellow slime mold—a science fiction fantasy that flows around its food to digest it; ruffled fungi in showy oranges and yellows; a common garden snake with two green stripes and red dots on its black scales.

Beating through a stretch of shoulder-high bracken fern was only a little scratchy. Fording the numerous streams was not a problem once I stopped the balancing act of boulder hopping, trying to stay dry, and simply waded across. But on the third day we came to a four-mile obstacle course of 36 blowdowns—towering trees that wind had brought crashing down on the path. The park's trail crew had not yet cut through these barriers with chain saws. Detouring around them meant negotiating massive snarls of logs and jungles of brush, a prospect more intimidating than clambering over or wriggling under the prostrate giants. In one maneuver, the ice ax strapped to my pack jabbed into the ground, pinning me underneath the tree. Saul and Phil tried tugging me out, but I was firmly snagged until I managed to slide out of my pack.

The going became easy as the forest thinned. Then it tapered into meadow, with only small stands of dwarf subalpine fir or mountain hemlock fringing the open ground. The subalpine fir's slender cone shape and the flexible branches of the mountain hemlock enable both these hardy, high-altitude species to shed the heavy snows near timberline—around 5,500 feet on the west side of the North Cascades. Some evergreens cross the timberline boundary, but they become so stunted they turn into gnarled, sprawling elfin shrubs called krummholz, a German word for crooked timber.

For two days we had been traveling in a tunnel of vegetation, our vistas gleaned from gaps in the forest or above the curtain of foliage. In what seemed like a few steps, we entered a vast open space and could gaze at a panorama of mountains, meadows, and sky.

Everywhere were contours carved by ice. The many-faceted mountains scalloped with hanging valleys and cirques, the sharp-crested ridges called arêtes, and the U-shaped trough descending Fisher Pass all bore the unmistakable signature of a glacier's hand.

There are more than 300 glaciers in the park—more than anywhere else in the United States except Alaska. These modern glaciers are mere ice cubes compared with the mammoth sheets, a mile thick, that once smothered the North Cascades plateau. Geologists say collisions of the earth's crustal plates created the tremendous pressures that pushed the plateau up from the bottom of an ancient sea. Alpine glaciers later carved it into a labyrinth of peaks and valleys. Volcanism less than a million years ago created Mount Baker and Glacier Peak, two huge volcanoes that stand just outside the park's boundaries and add glory to its vistas. Fisher Camp, where we would spend the night, was dominated by Mount Arriva, so close that we could hear the rocks clattering and chinking down its near-vertical buttress walls.

"Such falling rocks are a constant hazard. They're the heavy artillery that causes the most fatalities for climbers," said Saul, a man well qualified to speak about mountaineering in the North Cascades. He has climbed the highest peaks hundreds of times, spent countless hours finding routes across glaciers riddled with crevasses and icefalls, and passed days waiting out storms huddled in a tent. He worked for eight years as one of the two climbing rangers in the park, patrolling the more popular high routes and taking part in mountain rescues.

"There are always accidents—many of them a result of poor footing or rockfalls," he said. "With so much moisture and so much freezing and thawing, even granite surfaces fracture quickly into loose rocks. These are mountains that move.

"Weather is another hazard because it changes so fast, going from bright sun to a whiteout in an hour. Stumbling around on a ridge or a glacier when visibility is down to ten feet can be pretty dicey."

A S IF CUED by our conversation, sullen clouds surged in from the west, paused on the broad shoulders of Mount Logan, then roiled heavily across the sky. The sun vanished, and in the flat light the snow lost its sparkle. The air turned sharp and chill, but only a brief shower fell from the capricious sky.

Next morning, still in the cocoon of my sleeping bag, I peered at the day from the door of the tent. Mist reduced the world to ghostly silhouettes like those in Chinese paintings. As tatters of fog drifted across the mystic landscape, the shadows faded in and out of sight. Then bits of blue sky appeared on the horizon. "Sucker holes," Saul called them, "because they lure you out of the tent only to close over suddenly and send down a walloping storm."

But fickle alpine weather turned in our favor. The sky cleared, mists dissolved with magical speed, and shapes acquired color. The steep meadow leading to apparently misnamed Easy Pass basked in bright sunshine. Flowers spattered the green meadows like pigments in an abstract painting.

"All the blossoms look like they have lights on them," exclaimed Phil, bent over the timberline garden with his cameras. We were all brought to our knees by this flower show: lavender daisies, deep purple larkspur, lilac lupines, white yarrow, yellow violets, rosy pentstemon, and Indian paintbrush in a red so vivid it seemed to burn with an inner fire.

The colorful tapestry also lured butterflies. Most conspicuous were the mountain blues—small, pale creatures that fluttered low across the meadow like scraps of paper in the wind.

The climb to Easy Pass proved to be less arduous than it looked. The switchbacks tamed the steepness, and every time we paused we were cheered by a stunning view. On top of Easy Pass we had ascended into winter. Snow still covered the saddle itself and the north-facing slope on the other side. But the miracle of life had made inroads even on this high, white world. Patches of pink algae were in bloom, producing the curiosity known as watermelon snow.

Suncups were another phenomenon. They formed in places where wind-blown dust or pollen accumulated in irregularities on the surface. These dark spots absorb more heat and melt snow at a faster rate than surrounding areas. Then the dents, or cups, concentrate the sun's rays and grow larger until they scallop the surface like frothy meringue. Sometimes they grow so large they make walking wobbly and difficult, but they were not the problem that day. I was having trouble because the weight of my pack was pitching me forward on a slope so steep it verged on the vertical. My solution was unorthodox and not recommended, but what a sight it was when I sent my pack sliding down hundreds of feet, almost to the trees. My own descent then became a frolic in the slippery snow as I plunge-stepped down on my heels. One thrilling slide sent me headfirst a hundred yards downhill.

At the edge of greenness, where the wind carried the pungent aromas of the forest into the sterile purity of alpine air, we sat on some rocks savoring the warmth of the afternoon and the camaraderie of four days together on the trail.

For Saul such excursions into the wilderness are more than a quest for picture postcard scenes. He spoke of the euphoria that comes from experiencing nature on its own terms—the sharpening of senses dulled by daily routine and artifacts of technology. He believes the essence of the park lies in those totally wild realms of rock and ice, "where solitude and silence speak louder than the wind."

For me such distant, lofty summits are for gazing, but to experience one of those acclaimed high places, I set out to climb Mount Shuksan, a spectacular, glacier-clad giant in the northwest section of the park that has been called the showpiece of the North Cascades.

My first glimpse of Shuksan from the roadside was daunting. Below the naked rock pinnacle at the top, glaciers slashed with crevasses cascaded down the mountain. Great buttresses and sharp ridges pierced the crumpled, broken surface, creating an image of upheaval rendered in stone and ice. Though the summit stands at 9,131 feet, a midget by Himalayan standards, the mountain goes quickly from valley to summit, rearing almost straight up from a base about 2,650 feet high. So the eye sees an awesome vertical rise.

The Sulfide Glacier, on the south side of the mountain, offers the easiest of several routes to Shuksan's summit. Kathy Cosley, a petite blonde and, at 34, an outstanding *(Continued on page 26)*

*E*xploring the backcountry: On Thunder Creek Trail, naturalist Saul Weisberg (opposite) consults a field guide to identify the red-brown stalks of pinedrops, one of the nongreen plants that depend on fungi to synthesize their food. Using a hand lens, Saul takes a close-up look (left) at a western fence lizard. Fording a stream surging with snowmelt (below) provides a challenge for the author on a day hike to Boston Basin. Some 360 miles of trails lead into the park's wilderness of evergreen forests, glaciers, and jagged peaks.

JIM NELSON

*D*efying gravity, two mountaineers scale a wall on Sharkfin Tower above Boston Basin. Ropes, anchored by metal chocks wedged into cracks in the rock, provide a measure of protection. The Park Service advises also using helmets. Below the peaks that make the basin a magnet for climbers, a duo (above) crosses a glacier. Harbinger of spring, a glacier lily (below) blooms in the snow.

*C*hurned to a froth, Rainbow Falls (opposite) plummets 312 feet into the Stehekin River in the Lake Chelan National Recreation Area—one of the three parts of the park complex. Its myriad waterfalls gave the Cascade Range its name. Rapids of the Skagit River (above) bring adventure to rafters on a run through the Ross Lake National Recreation Area. A section of the North Cascades Highway traverses this unit, providing easy access to lakes for fishing and boating. At one of the highway's scenic overlooks a visitor (right) provides a perch for a chipmunk.

professional alpine guide, led the way up. Like Saul, she is one of those people who would rather risk a rockfall or avalanche than ride a tram to a peak overrun with people.

The Sulfide route did not require the skills and hardware of a technical climb, but it was steep. At first we had to battle through brush that tugged at our packs. Then at timberline our pace slowed to the plodding monotony of kicking steps into the still-hard July snow.

Hours spent sweating in shorts and T-shirts in the bright sunshine were followed by an afternoon storm that assailed us with biting winds and thick clouds. Fog obliterated our vertical world.

We camped at 6,000 feet on the glacier. The rain drumming against the tarp, the wind flailing the tent, and the sputtering flame of the butane stove lulled me to sleep before supper. The clamminess inside the tent woke me after an hour.

"When you're camped on snow, the floor sweats. It's like a plastic bag on a block of ice," explained Kathy.

The rain had stopped. Pink clouds scudded past the ragged crests of the Northern Pickets pressing into the pale, opalescent sky. Before long the light seeped away and the mountains lost their sharpness, but the snow glimmering in the moonlight mellowed the dark frostiness of the night.

"A view like this is payment for the pain," declared Kathy. "I also enjoy testing my endurance and ability. I like feeling the strength in my legs. And to reach the top is tremendously exhilarating."

*S*OMETIME around midnight the rain resumed. Water seeped into my down sleeping bag, which is useless when wet, so that the buzz of Kathy's alarm clock at 4 a.m. was almost welcome.

We headed up the glacier, muffled in fog that permeated the silence with its melancholy. The clear, sweet warble of a rosy finch chimed across the silence, sounding a startling but cheerful note in the emptiness. These intrepid birds eat benumbed insects blown up onto the snow and also feed on ice worms. It was hard to believe such improbable creatures as ice worms really exist, even when Kathy pointed to the inch-long squiggles on the surface. Biologists have determined that they are a kind of freshwater worm that has moved higher and higher up the mountains. Now these tiny worms inhabit glaciers, swimming in the meltwater between the ice crystals and surviving on wind-borne pollen. No one really knows what happens to the ice worms in winter.

Briefly the fog lifted, and billowing white clouds appeared, soaring upward like mountains against a surly gray sky. A few plodding footsteps later the world vanished once again from view.

Kathy recommended that we turn back to the tent if it didn't clear by 9:30 a.m. It would not be safe to go much higher in the fog. Waiting back at camp for a break in the weather to continue the climb meant at least another night in a damp tent, shivering in a down bag that had not dried. The prospect weakened my resolve, and I opted for going all the way down. It is small consolation that being "weathered out" is considered a true North Cascades experience.

An easier outing, and one of the most popular day hikes in the park, is the trail to Cascade Pass in the southern sector. In less than 4 miles the path climbs from 3,600 to 5,384 feet, ascending into a mountain spectacle that steals your breath away. One afternoon I spiraled up the 36 switchbacks, accompanied by the joyful sounds of water foaming against rock. Another companion, never out of sight, was massive Johannesburg Mountain, towering over the narrow valley of the Cascade River. An overcast hung above the broad summit so that its snowfields and hanging glaciers seemed to be spilling out of the clouds. From time to time glaciers rumbled as chunks of ice broke off the mountain's sheer face.

About 30 hikers had arrived at Cascade Pass that day, according to the tally of Jim Ohlsten, the backcountry ranger posted there for the summer. Over the season there might be as many as 5,000, less than the number of visitors to Yosemite's Tuolumne Meadows on a weekend. But hikers and horseback riders had been coming to the pass before the park was created in 1968, and the traffic, campsites, and fire pits had eroded the fragile meadows.

To restore the area, the Park Service had roped off the damaged meadows and embarked on a pioneer revegetation program based on field studies by Joe and Margaret Miller—avid hikers and botanists who became full-time volunteers. The reclamation project has demonstrated that subalpine plants can be grown from seed in a greenhouse and then transplanted to high elevations.

Long before Cascade Pass became a hiker's destination, it had been a heavily used trading route for prehistoric Indians. From the west of the mountains came shells, dried clams, obsidian, fish oil, and mountain goat wool. These were bartered for dried deer and elk meat, along with dried salmon and animal skins from the east.

To the Indians the North Cascades were the realm of the gods. Today in the southeast corner of the park complex, there are other inhabitants who have also forged a special bond with the land. The 100 or so year-round residents of the Stehekin Valley live close to nature and interact with the land and the seasons in an intimate way. Porcupines waddle past windows, bear cubs raid vegetable gardens, bald eagles skim the lake, and cougars pad through the deep powder of winter.

Stehekin is a place where people bake bread, fires crackle in wood stoves, and the store is a four-hour boat ride away. If something breaks down, you fix it yourself. Isolation and long, snowy winters have created an independent life-style, in which old-fashioned skills and pioneer traditions of self-sufficiency are kept alive. There is no high school, and no way to get there by car. Residents will tell you that the lack of telephones, TV, and other amenities makes their community unique, and they would like to keep it that way.

Like most people, I arrived in Stehekin by passenger boat, boarding at the town of Chelan and traveling four hours on a 50-mile-long finger of water that stretches between mountains most of its length. Lake Chelan sits prettily in a deep, glacier-gouged trough that plunges more than 400 feet below sea level.

*B*OATS HAVE BROUGHT summer vacationers to Stehekin as far back as in the 1890s. A display at the Park Service visitor center at Stehekin Landing describes the old three-story Field Hotel, which had a ballroom, a candelabra in the lobby, and Brussels carpets on the floors. In those days visitors came with parasols, cameras, fishing poles, and sketchbooks. They also carried guns, for the mountain goats were so numerous along the lake that "men shot them from rowboats just to hear the splash." The streams were said to have been so full of trout "you had to hide behind a tree to bait a hook."

The day was warm and sunny as I bicycled up the valley, but the afternoon winds, cooled by the mountain snows, swooped down on the lake, rippling the surface with whitecaps. Mergansers chugged along in the water undisturbed, and ospreys dived for trout. Boughs of western red cedar with their sprays of lacy foliage dangled gracefully above the gravel road to the Stehekin Valley Ranch.

The rustic resort, with its cabins with canvas roofs and kerosene lamps, enables owner Clifford Courtney, age 35, to make ends meet and stay on in the valley where his grandfather had hacked a homestead out of the forest 80 years ago.

"The ranch is nothing fancy, but that's part of my screening process. Those folks that can stand my facilities are the kind of outdoor people I want as clientele," said Cliff, an amiable host who enjoys talking to guests at the long log tables in the dining room.

Near the ranch stands the 16-by-20-foot cabin where Cliff and his five older brothers lived from 1961 to 1967. "The folks slept downstairs, and we were in the loft above," said Cliff as he led me inside. Though the cast-iron cooking range, galvanized tub, treadle sewing machine, and wooden yoke for carrying pails of water belonged to a bygone era, they were part of yesterday for Cliff.

"I made spending money trapping beaver and marten in winter—that was my allowance. It was also a great way to learn about the environment—interacting with it, using it, but not abusing it. I trapped for 16 years, even after the park came in 1968; it was part of our life-style. Now it's against the law.

"Congress placed the Stehekin Valley in the Lake Chelan Na-tional Recreation Area, instead of in the park itself, because the legisla-tors recognized our unique culture and the need for our community to continue to exist. But the Park Service has been putting more and more restrictions on our activities.

"Back in the sixties, people here wanted the park to take over because they were afraid of large-scale logging, and now these anacon-da tactics are squeezing the life out of the community."

The park disagrees with Cliff's interpretation of Congress's in-tentions and insists it is merely trying to regulate the community's "considerably expanded" commercial operations. Perhaps it was inev-itable that the longtime residents of the valley would feel threatened by the regulations of the Park Service. Many of them had come to Ste-hekin to find a place where they were beyond the reach of the govern-ment and could do things their own way. Old-timers like Curt Courtney, Cliff's uncle, look back with nostalgia on the years when they could do what they wanted.

"The state's hunting season in September came too early for us because we had no refrigeration to store the meat. So some of us would declare another deer season in January. Now you think of something you want to do, and you run into a battery of permits."

While rugged individualism characterizes Stehekin, solitude is the essence of Desolation Peak. A hike to that summit with backcoun-try ranger Kelly Bush and Phil Schofield was a good way to say good-bye to the park.

Images of Desolation Peak crowd my memory. Panoramas stretching away to every horizon. The luster of crimson Indian paint-brush blooming beside the gritty darkness of granite. Cicadas chirping in a field exploding with purple lupines. Mountains in the morning mist with their snow peaks shining in the sun. A grouse sitting on the shutters of the old fire lookout cabin where we spent the night.

There is a logbook in the cabin, and I remember an entry by Helen Counts, a 19-year-old student from Virginia. "I feel most fortu-nate to be here, as if I've finally been let in on a big secret of nature. To think that this has existed for so long in all its beauty...."

There is also pleasure in knowing that for many tomorrows all that beauty will still be there.

FOLLOWING PAGES: Trekking above the clouds at sunset, climbers head past double-crested Whatcom Peak. Roped up, they use ice axes to probe for crevasses on the Challenger Glacier.

JOHN DITTLI

JOHNNY JOHNSON / DRK PHOTO

JEFF GNASS

Below glacier-carved heights dominated by massive Mount Redoubt, a backpacker strides through a meadow on Copper Ridge Trail. Familiar sight in the high country, a hoary marmot (above) munches a mountain avens. During the harsh winter this creature hibernates in its burrow. Rich hues of the Sitka columbine (top right) help the plant compete for pollinators during the short growing season. Red spots on the Columbia lily also lure pollinating insects.

*G*randeur of western red cedars, soaring 200 feet or
more above the lowland forest floor, awes a hiker on the Big Beaver
Trail. These giant trees took root as much as a thousand years ago,
flourishing in the moist soils on the west side of the Cascades, where
humid winds from the Pacific bring abundant rain. Inhabitant of
conifer forests, the great gray owl raises its chicks in a nest of twigs.
Large, sharp teeth enable a porcupine to gnaw the bark from a tree
for the sap and cambium underneath.

Knife-edge ridges and precipices too steep to hold snow guard the Picket Range,

a remote, formidable wilderness accessible only to skilled mountaineers.

Voyageurs
Pathway to the Interior

By Seymour L. Fishbein
Photographs by Jay Dickman and Richard Olsenius

WE HAD PADDLED EAST across Rainy Lake, in kinks and doodles and long, plodding reaches, as canoes often do on gruff, broad waters where distant contours fuse in a hazy green smear. We slalomed around a few islands near shore and some of the boundary-line buoys out in the open, with apologies to Canada for breaching its border. Now, in narrower Namakan Lake, the course looked much clearer, but the powerboats were closer and making waves, and the shores, more distinct, revealed a cottage and a dock here and there. It does not take much of that to make a back-country canoeist feel squeezed; some of us were heard to grumble.

Esther Kellogg, that rarity among paddlers, a non-grumbler, stroked gently over the ripples of discontent. She remembered other times, other places: the Boundary Waters wilderness and Canada's Quetico country just to the east—remote, enchanting, but long famous, reservations-only places. In contrast, Esther observed in her soft-spoken manner, "when you want to come here, you just come."

Just for the joy of being wanted in a national park, try Voyageurs, one of the youngest, yet rich in some of the most ancient earth history. We hear much of saturated parklands, of America's crown jewels being loved to death. Here is one that needs more loving, and is worthy of it. You will share sunsets with brooding eagles, glide by loons cackling and bobbing on the waters, awake to birdsong, and hike with the woodland choir through the long summer days. Pick berries, few or many as the fickle seasons decree—if the black bears don't get to them first. Pitch camp at more than a hundred designated sites, or anywhere else along miles of lakeshore, without reservation, without registration, without a fee; build a campfire and await the green shimmer of northern lights and the howling of wolves in the witching hours. No charge either for the use of a dozen park-owned

A black bear cub checks out a downed limb near a campground in Voyageurs National Park. More than 150 bears roam the park.

PRECEDING PAGES: Woods and rock and water, some 218,000 acres' worth, make Voyageurs a paradise for boating—in craft ranging from power cruisers to houseboats, sightseeing boats, and bobbing canoes.

ERWIN & PEGGY BAUER (OPPOSITE); MATT BRADLEY (PRECEDING PAGES)

VOYAGEURS
NATIONAL PARK

LOCATION: Minnesota
ESTABLISHED: April 8, 1975
SIZE: 218,054 acres

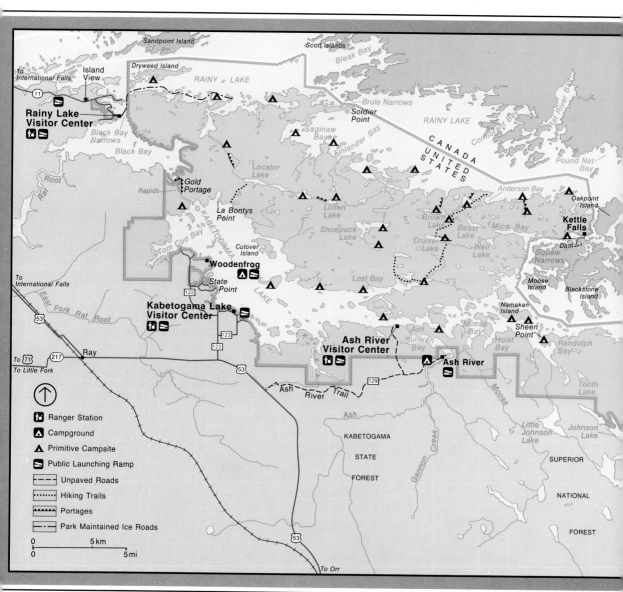

canoes and open boats on six interior lakes, some of them especially esteemed for their fish: largemouth bass, crappie, muskellunge.

Summer visitors can explore only the park edges by car. To get inside requires something that floats—powerboat, sailboat, floatplane, or canoe—on four big, island-peppered lakes traveled by the French-Canadian fur traders for whom the park is named. There were no roads here in the time of the voyageurs, the 17th to the 19th centuries. There are none now, save for the fading spoor of the tote roads hacked through the wilderness when "cut-out-and-get-out" logging arrived around the turn of this century.

Walleye and northern pike and other fish in these lakes have filled the nets of commercial fishermen and fed Native Americans, voyageurs, loggers, miners, and mill hands. The vast expanse of the larger lakes also attracted powerboats long before the park was born. "You can enjoy canoeing here," Superintendent Ben Clary told me, "but Voyageurs is basically a motorboating park."

Most Voyageurs traffic seems to concur. In this, today's visitors, swiftly gobbling up the miles in outboards or sleek cruisers or, more sedately, in boxy houseboats, are probably more faithful to the spirit of the voyageurs than I, who prefer canoes. The voyageurs spent unrelenting days at the paddles and labored under portage loads of 180 pounds, sometimes 300 pounds or more. They knew what it meant to "live hard, lie hard, sleep hard, eat dogs"—and they surely would have favored the easier life of a mechanized age. Still, these lakes are now a national park, commemorating the exploits of those canoemen. Paddling offered the more seemly way to explore it.

Making no secret of such sentiments, I was soon in touch with Martin Kellogg, a St. Paul manufacturer of precision plastics. Martin thinks that for real enjoyment—to keep in touch with water, land, and sky—canoes are the *only* way to go. I can hear him in an old voyageurs' chorale: "The plowman loves his cart, the hunter loves his gun, his hound; The musician loves his music; me, my canoe—it's everything to me."

Martin enlisted Esther, his wife and bowperson; his son Joe; and Joanne Peterson, Joe's wife and bowperson. One sparkling summer morning we set out near the Rainy Lake Visitor Center on an itinerary that would traverse three of the four big lakes, a 75-mile circumnavigation of the Kabetogama Peninsula, heartland of the park. For this voyage, the Kelloggs uncached the family jewels.

We had converged from opposite poles of the canoeing world. I am bonded to early Grumman aluminum—a scarred 17-footer acquired, at second hand, in the 1950s. Martin is a collector, with an eye for the beauty and feel of a canoe, its materials, its pedigree. He and Esther and I launched in their honey-hued "woodie," a spacious 19-footer made by a St. Paul high school senior. The gifted young builder had shaped it of half-inch-wide cedar strips glued edge to edge. A transparent coating of fiberglass and epoxy allows the light cedar tones to shine through. Joe and Joanne paddled the Kelloggs' green Seliga, a 17-foot wood-and-canvas thoroughbred made by the octogenarian craftsman Joe Seliga, in Ely, Minnesota.

Heading north, we threaded the Black Bay Narrows, then turned east and settled in for a 2½-day, 35-mile pull through Rainy Lake—also called Lac la Pluie on bilingual Canadian maps. It rains here all right, in torrents at times, but the name derives from *koo-chiching,* a Cree Indian term referring to the mist rising above the falls that roared on the Rainy River 11 miles to the west. Early in the century a power dam buried the falls; today the turbines power the Boise Cascade Corporation paper mills at International Falls, Minnesota, and its cross-river neighbor, Fort Frances, Ontario. Rainy Lake and all the other large lakes of Voyageurs are reservoirs, rising and falling to meet the needs of the mills and other priorities decreed by the United States and Canada.

A flight of white pelicans idled high above us, shifting formations without seeming purpose, from column to file to rough V's. These bulky birds, among the largest waterbird species in North America with wings spanning nine feet, visit Voyageurs for the fishing; they nest elsewhere.

A dark rectangle at waterline on Bushyhead Island reminded us of the short-lived gold rush here. The fever struck in 1893; super-heated hopefuls rushed in on foot, by dogsled, and by train. The richest of seven mines yielded about 4,600 dollars' worth of gold. Today, bats and mosquitoes populate the waterlogged shaft on Bushyhead.

*T*HE ISLAND got its name, reported a boomtown journal, "because it rises boldly out of the lake . . . and is crowned with a luxuriant growth of pine timber, giving it 'a bushy appearance, an emerald set in a sea of glass.' " This sea has a thousand islands, 600 of them within Voyageurs, most of them bushy-headed emeralds. They do not sort out easily; a break that seems to scribe an island profile may turn out to be an indentation leading to a cul-de-sac—and a tiresome doubling back. Reading map and compass and island patterns, we reach a variety of conclusions. Some, such as mine, are tinged with fantasy; others' less so, Joanne's least of all.

Though I did not note it then, the Rainy Lake emeralds have more than bushy heads in common. A week later Lee Grim, science instructor at Rainy River Community College and a summer park biologist, pointed out as we spread the map that groups of islands have similar shapes and lie in rough alignment, like schools of fish. "See how they're oriented northeast-southwest," he observed. In this pattern geologists have read a fragment of earth history written 2.7 billion years ago, when crustal plates came together from north and south and pushed up mountains. The islands are the relics of those ancient mountain-building forces, explained Lee. The granites and schists and greenstones here lie near the southern edge of the Canadian Shield, the oldest basement rock in North America.

Somewhat to the discomfort of Joanne, our navigating whiz, we often kept track by the numbers, checking those on the map against the ones on the flat-topped can buoys and the pointed nun buoys. Many of the buoys mark the U. S.–Canadian border. The voyageurs shaped the contour of the two nations here. After decades of dispute, statesmen laid the boundary along this accustomed fur-trade route, which ran to the northwest where the richest trove of beaver peltry lay, and eastward to Grand Portage, the rendezvous depot at Minnesota's northeastern tip.

Guidebook wisdom warns: Beware the winds of Rainy Lake. Northwesters sweep down, driving impossible waves, funneling to a climax in the Brule Narrows; just beyond, we are promised, await the shelter and tranquil waters of Saginaw Bay. For us Rainy Lake was simply a humdrum grind—until Saginaw Bay. There a southerly wind met us face on and scalloped the bay with whitecaps. An old story. *"C'est le vent frivolant . . . qui vole, qui frivole,"* sang the voyageurs. "It's the frivolous wind . . . which flies, which plays about."

The frivolous wind forced a mean two-mile pull until we found shelter and sweet repose on Little Finlander Island. Not counting the doodling, we had put 17 miles of Rainy Lake behind us, a tiring day—not to be confused with a voyageur's day. One chronicler reported a day on Lake Superior when the canoemen paddled from 3 a.m. to 9:30 p.m., 57,600 strokes for a distance of 79 miles. "No human beings except the Canadian French could stand this," wrote traveler Thomas L. McKenney. And not just any Canadian French: "If . . . he shall reach five feet ten or eleven, it forever excludes him from the privilege of becoming voyageur. There is no room for the legs of such people, in these canoes. But if he shall stop growing at about five feet four inches, and be gifted with a good voice . . . he is considered as having been born under a most favorable star." Voyageur songs, rhythmically complementing paddling, eased the toil; a good voice brought extra pay.

Good voices sang for us at Little Finlander, a melancholy tune with drawn-out notes, the lethargy of summertime. *Poor Sam Peabody Peabody Peabody,* sang the white-throated sparrows. So goes the rendering south of the border; to the north people may hear it as *Sweet Sweet Canada Canada Canada.* I heard the melody wherever I camped or hiked in the park—but never saw the singers.

From Little Finlander we slipped through Kempton Channel, keeping a barrier of islands between us and the broad bulk of eastern Rainy Lake. Lumbering great blue herons and soaring herring gulls and swift cormorants coursed the skies; on the water, tight broods of ducklings swarmed around merganser parents. Once, when we passed perhaps 30 yards from a lone loon swimming, Joanne greeted it with a creditable loon call. The bird rose swiftly to its full length on the water and beat its wings. A courtship dance, I suggested, congratulating Joanne for making a connection. Her good mimicry had indeed struck a chord, though not the one I imagined. The loon, I later learned, had risen in a threat response, defending its domain.

Loons breed in Voyageurs with mixed success. I saw chicks in Rainy Lake, where the reservoir levels rise and fall less than did the natural cycles of the lake. In the other large lakes—Namakan, Sand Point, and Kabetogama—reservoir levels rise and fall more steeply; the loons' lakeside nests often get swamped. "We have yet to see a chick hatch in those lakes this year," I was told by Larry Kallemeyn, the park's aquatic research biologist, in midsummer of 1991. Reservoir levels in some years also impact the spawning of walleyes and northern pike, both of major interest to the sportfishing community.

The turbines at International Falls, owned by Boise Cascade, annually produce some five million dollars' worth of electricity for the mills. Dams operate under rules set by a joint U. S.–Canadian commission, which considers hydropower, water supplies, and pollution control, among other needs. Proposals to better meet the needs of loons and fish have been under study for years.

OUR SECOND DAY ended at the edge of Anderson Bay. An evening on the granite bluffs above the bay offers one of the scenic joys of Voyageurs. From there the emerald islands fall away in silhouette on a great silver sea against a western sky of rose and lavender. From our low-lying rocky spit, we saw some of that, but there was no joy in it, for we came under siege by a ravenous army of flies. No one could explain their numbers or their fury—perhaps the unaccustomed warm spell, or an unusual hatch. The flies found the skin edges where repellent or socks or collars or shirtsleeves ended; they piled on our clothing, one atop the other in thick mounds. We plunged into the lake; when we came up for air, they were in our hair, on our faces and necks. Mercifully, a night wind shooed the vicious horde; reborn, we stretched out on our rock and ended the day's birdwatching with a long, languid look at Cygnus, the Swan, twinkling across the heavens.

We took a long noontime break the next day at our first portage, Kettle Falls, to tour the famous—or infamous—historic hotel of the same name. Here came dam builders, loggers, fishermen, tourists—and bootleggers and prostitutes. In recent years the park has renovated and refurbished the old hostelry as a park concession and made additional improvements; it was awaiting a new operator and was closed when we visited. With a caretaker escort we wandered through it, slowing understandably at the bar, which was filled with memorabilia; these included a half dozen portraits from the 1920s, '30s, and '40s of scrumptious nudes—idealized models, not the working girls of Kettle Falls—all recalling the liveliness of yesteryear. Park officials consider the hotel, with its history and its crossroads location, a significant landmark. It reopened in 1992.

Joe and Martin Kellogg hefted the canoes, and the rest of us hauled the packs and gear over the few hundred yards of portage trail. We then proceeded south and westward through Namakan Narrows and into Kabetogama. Powerboats often throttled back, to avoid making waves for us; some raced by; a few hooted, mocking our strokes. Near one island a motorboat suddenly cut a tight arc and sped toward us. "Be careful!" a voice called out. "A bear is swimming in the middle of the lake." Wolf Dieter Freude, a pharmacist from Langenhagen, Germany, and his wife and two daughters had been touring the park. In their rented 16-foot launch they had no fear of the black bear, but oh, those frail-looking canoes, they must be warned. We smiled, thanked them—and hurried for the spot they had left. In the jargon of wildlife management, bears are classified as charismatic megafauna; people run to, not away from them. We got only a distant peek as the bear emerged from the lake and wandered into the woodland.

We hoped to hike up into the Kabetogama Peninsula and explore interior lakes in the park canoes there, until a wind roughed up the waters around our Sheep Islands camp. We were windbound, *dégradés,* the voyageurs would have said; so we snoozed, swatted bugs, listened to the maples and aspens hiss and groan and the surf beat against the shore—a day the Lotus Eaters might have envied. Not all that degrading, as it turned out.

Though we missed the interior lakes that day, I was no stranger to some of them. In late winter, which is still midwinter here in northernmost Minnesota, I had joined Jerry Snyker and members of the Voyageurs Region National Park Association, a volunteer support group, for some cross-country skiing. We set out on a day that dawned at 11° below zero Fahrenheit, with a windchill factor of minus 40. Not to worry, we'll be in the woods where there's no wind, said Snyker. An addicted marathoner, he will ski 22 miles to a restaurant to meet his wife, who has driven there. We skied a few miles of county and state land to the park edge, on a trail built by Jerry and the Polar Polers ski club of International Falls. We drove out on the park-plowed ice road in the cold glare of a scanting, ungenerous *(Continued on page 56)*

*B*reaking camp during a 6-day, 75-mile circumnavigation of Kabetogama Peninsula, author Sy Fishbein (white hat) helps steady a cedar canoe while companions load gear. The 19-foot "woodie" was built by a high school senior. Crew mates include (from left) excursion leader Martin Kellogg, daughter-in-law Joanne Peterson, and son Joe. As in voyageur times, watercraft are the chief form of transportation here. A houseboat (opposite) sedately navigates the narrows of Black Bay.

*B*ounty from the lake garnishes a mouth-watering feast.
Onetime logger and trapper, Laverne Oveson today keeps his hand in as
a fishing guide. Here, on Lake Kabetogama, his wife, Lucille, helps him
prepare a sizzling repast of pan-fried walleye, beans, and potatoes—a
"shore dinner," as locals call it. "I still get a kick out of catching fish,"
says the veteran outdoorsman. "It still feels the same to me as it did 30
years ago." Prized for their walleye, the park's lakes also support
abundant pike and smallmouth bass. But mercury contamination in
some of the lakes—particularly in large fish—is cause for concern, as it
is in many other northern U. S. and Canadian lakes.

*F*ly-in anglers, using their floatplane as a fishing platform, try for bass

in the mirrored waters of one of the park's 26 smaller lakes.

JOHN & ANN MAHAN (ABOVE AND BELOW)

*S*treaks *of milky*
quartz thread ancient
bedrock along the shore of
Rainy Lake. Here, on the edge
of the Canadian Shield,

exposed rock dates back 2.7 billion years. Voyageurs provides a habitat for some 275 bird and mammal species. The "dancing" loon (opposite) may be trying to divert attention from its nest nearby with a display of aggression. The park's largest mammal, a moose, munches contentedly on aquatic plants. About 200 of these animals roam Voyageurs.

sun, past ice fishermen patiently waiting beside their holes, to ski the
Black Bay Trail. We chose a hilly, curvy six-mile run through groves of
white and red pine and black spruce and aspen—one of which stood
in my path at the bottom of a slope and stopped me cold. Not for my
skill but for my bruises, I felt entitled to be called *hivernant,* which
signified a tough, veteran voyageur who overwintered in the wilderness. The word has a fine, adventurous cachet—much more appealing
than the name given to novices who wintered back east; *mangeurs de
lard*—pork-eaters—they were called, deriding the softer life that went
with their diet of salt pork and dried corn or peas.

My companions thought Voyageurs could use more ski trails
and have spent much effort seeking to persuade park officials to this
view. Snowmobiles, however, are more popular here. At the invitation
of the park I mounted one and sped out to the peninsula and down a
few of the lakes. The snow machine makes a wonderful winter beast of
burden, a great improvement on the horse or reindeer. As a recre-
ational conveyance through national park backcountry, however, it
stirs controversy. Legislation establishing Voyageurs authorized the
continued use of snowmobiles; local people insist on them as the tra-
ditional means of access, and because they attract visitors. This concern over tourism is exceptionally delicate since, I heard repeatedly,
Voyageurs visitation has never matched Park Service projections.

*M*ARTIN KELLOGG, a leader of the
Voyageurs Region National Park Association, joined the effort to create
the park back in the 1960s, as part of a campaign to promote Minnesota tourism. In time he felt the force and eloquence of Ernest Ober-
holtzer and Sigurd Olson and others who spoke for the wilderness—
wilderness where mankind treads lightly. A year ago Martin was offered a snowmobile tour of the park, in the hope that he would under-
stand better the snowmobilers' point of view and the proposal for a
snowmobile trail down the Kabetogama Peninsula. He declined. "I
told them," he recalled, " 'You've got to be crazy. I wouldn't touch that
with a ten-foot pole.' A snowmobile trail there would amount to putting in a narrow-gauge road. We know some snowmobiling is authorized in the legislation, but it should be limited to the major lakes."
Snowmobiling continues on Kabetogama Peninsula while the Park Service considers proposals to define the wilderness there.

My winter outing in March had coincided with the first arrival
of bald eagles, beginning their preparations for the breeding season.
Now, during our midsummer voyage, dark-headed eaglets the size of
their parents were about to take wing. On our fifth night out, the last,
we lucked onto the fine Northland campsite, hemmed by islands,
shaded by thick sprays of white pine, visited by nuthatches, warblers,

and hummingbirds, enhanced by bright red raspberries, which Martin gleefully harvested. On an island just offshore, two bulky fledgling eagles perched on a limb not far from a sprawling platform nest. The snowy-headed parents perched in nearby trees, their breeding season, to all appearances, a success.

Or was it? "It appears we may have a problem with our eagles," Larry Kallemeyn told me a few days later. "Blood and feather samples from fledglings show PCB levels as high as anything that's been documented in the Great Lakes, which have a known problem. Our information is preliminary, but it is scary, because we have no idea where this stuff is coming from." At high enough levels, the toxic pollutant can inhibit breeding or produce deformed young.

In addition to PCBs, mercury has been found in Voyageurs' eagles and in fish in park lakes—a hazard noted in thousands of U. S. and Canadian lakes. The Minnesota Department of Health has published a booklet describing the health risks of contaminants and recommending guidelines for eating fish from the lakes tested; these include several in the park, where researchers are seeking to pinpoint the sources of mercury.

A few miles beyond our Northland campsite, we hauled the boats and packs over the tiny neck known as Gold Portage. Watery fingers lead to and from the portage, tranquil, reedy streams thick with mallards and mergansers and sandpipers. We entered Black Bay, where white pelicans calmly trolled, dipping now and then to scoop a fish—much less frenzied than the kamikaze feeding dives of their kin, the brown pelicans.

Just beyond that quiet corner, about three miles from home, Black Bay turned tiger, chopped by a fierce wind against us. We laid up on a sheltered shore and sat it out for three hours; then, tired of waiting, we pushed off into the teeth of it. On quiet waters the third person in the woodie could relax, birdwatch, photograph—"duffin'," the Kelloggs called it. Nobody dared loaf now, as we bounced on top, off the sides, and into the trough of waves that crested two feet or more. No matter how swiftly we stroked, shores off our beam seemed to stand still. Several times we scuttled into patches of high grasses to take a breather. We filtered water through a bandana and gulped it—a crude, some would say risky, technique, but it was all we had and our thirst was huge. In this manner we crept wearily across until, within the arc of the mainland, we found quiet water. So ended our 75-mile voyage, the crew and canoes well worn, but none the worse for it.

Within a few days I set off again, this time more in the style of a *coureur de bois,* which means "woods runner" and in voyageur days was an epithet for the free-lance, unlicensed traders who roamed the wilderness. Biologist Lee Grim, photographer Richard Olsenius, and I backpacked across the eastern end of the Kabetogama Peninsula, some ten trail miles from Lost Bay to Anderson Bay. This is land the glaciers scrubbed down to bare rock; much of it is still exposed, granite and schist. When the ice sheets retreated some 12,000 years ago, green growth and birds and insects and mammals—the grand web we call the boreal forest—claimed the land.

In the early decades of this century, loggers harvested more than 100 million board feet of sawtimber on the peninsula. White pine went first for, unlike denser species, it floats. The logs were sleigh-hauled over the frozen lakes to hoisting depots, or piled on the ice to await the spring thaw, when they were chained up into great log islands and floated to the hoists. Bustling logging camps sprouted and, when the surrounding forest was gone, moved on.

As the sawtimber declined the loggers went for pulpwood—balsam, birch, the hitherto scorned aspen (or poplar, known as popple hereabouts). With the blessing of progress giant machines chopped pulp trees into chips and blew them into trucks. In 1971, the year the park was authorized, Boise Cascade cut 3,000 cords of wood on the Kabetogama Peninsula.

*T*ODAY GREEN LIFE and wildlife surge back. Bracken and impatient young trees choke old logging roads, and beavers drown them. We watched beavers swim, skirted their ponds, admired their dams and lodges. Beavers were nearly extirpated here early in the century; now hundreds range the peninsula. Their engineering has transformed 13 percent of the land; good dam sites are growing scarce.

Yet for all their energy and skill, the beavers' world is not without its hazards. We saw leaky dams and collapsed ones. And beavers are fair prey. "They suffer from house raids by otters," said Lee as we looked over a weed-topped lodge. Wolves take a toll in summer, though winter seems to frustrate them. "You see tracks on the snow converging on the lodge from all directions," Lee continued. "The wolves sniff around the breathing hole, but there's no way they can get at the beavers, and they back off and walk away."

A broad-winged hawk sailed around a lake; ravens played the air currents. Lee communed with a golden-crowned kinglet, exchanging thin *tsee* calls with the unseen bird. We heard the much shriller call of a wood duck, swimming with her brood on a beaver pond; Lee tried the same tack, but she was in no mood for small talk as she crisply paddled off with her ducklings.

We passed by the aromatic flowering shrub called sweet fern, which Lee gathers outside the park to perfume his sauna, and the astringent sweet gale banked along a lakeshore; we passed wildflowers in bloom—pearly everlasting, blue asters, tiny lavender harebells. It did not take long for the woodland sorcery to capture us. Less than a half mile from the big, busy waters of Voyageurs we sat by a dark, quiet lake hemmed by billowing granite knobs, by evergreens and birch and aspen—with not a house, not a dock, not a boat anywhere in sight. "I would like to sit here," mused Richard, "and see the first snowfall. I would like to see the first ice form and break up into wavelets." We sat long enough to see a loon splash in for a landing.

Geologists call this glaciated, undulating land "swell-and-swale" topography. We hiked beside bogs of sphagnum moss and tamarack, beneath waterfalls plunging into lily pools, over high windy ledges, across rocks hoared with lichens. Lee Grim has a special liking for lichens, and a patch of tiny, red-topped British soldiers and bright green pixie cups stopped us in our tracks as he held forth. The park boasts 400 kinds of lichens, including generous supplies of *Cladonia*, known as caribou moss. Caribou may nibble up to 12 pounds of it in a day's foraging. There are no caribou here now to gnaw the lichens from the rocks, but there were once and may be again. Pete Gogan, the park's ungulate biologist, told me that the park has looked at restocking. One problem is the deer, which carry a brainworm parasite—harmless to the host—that invariably kills caribou.

For much of our route across the peninsula we followed old logging roads, in places so overgrown that even Lee, who helped lay out the park trails, had to rely on markers to find the way. Midway in our hike we camped at Cruiser Lake, whose name recalls the logging days when timber cruisers assessed the size and value of forest stands. A logging camp once stood across the lake; we hiked around to see what was left: some chimney work, rusted metal. Out of the hulk of a camp stove, a tall aspen grew.

Near Cruiser, a few years ago, my friends Bud and Fran Heinselman of St. Paul saw a few wolves appear, then vanish. Bud tried howling—and six wolves sauntered out of the woods onto a rock ledge, a rare, unforgettable sight, a just reward for a couple who have devoted their lifetime together to the wilderness. Some twenty wolves, in three packs, range the peninsula. Lee and Richard heard a few of them howl one night.

Less than a half century ago naysayers scorned the Kabetogama Peninsula as "a worthless rock pile." Now, on this land and along its shores we hear the howling of wolves, the cackling of loons, sparrow songs, the cry of eagles on the wind—"all that is worth listening for," as Sigurd Olson taught us.

FOLLOWING PAGES: Reeds and birch trees line the shore of Rainy Lake, the park's largest body of water. Elsewhere, steep bluffs and rock outcroppings give a bolder edge to the 350-square-mile lake.

JEFF GNASS

*A*utumn displays its magic amid the trees and mosses of the great north woods. Afternoon sun (opposite) filters through a stand of white birch and maples, whose fallen leaves (below) lend color to a carpet of moss. A green ribbon of unlogged conifers at water's edge (above) screens a logged-over, second-growth forest of deciduous trees.

*P*ark for all seasons, Voyageurs bustles with life even as winter spreads its cloak of snow and ice. A boy on snowshoes takes his dogs for a romp on frozen Sand Point Lake at the park's eastern border. Nearby, his father dips a line into a fishing hole augered through the ice. Each winter, some 45,000 visitors enjoy park activities that range from cross-country skiing to snowmobiling (bottom right). An ice road,

maintained by the park, gives access to ice fishing sites and sweeping vistas on Rainy Lake and to ski trails that dip and rise on Kabetogama Peninsula. Such pastimes are a far cry from the days of the fur trade, when only trappers and seasoned voyageurs ranged these winter woodlands. Freeze-up called a halt to water travel, and many canoemen already had paddled their pelts back to civilization.

JAY DICKMAN (ALL)

Theodore Roosevelt
Dakota Adventure

By Jennifer C. Urquhart
Photographs by Michael Melford

"*T*HE GRASS-LAND stretches out in the sunlight like a sea," wrote Theodore Roosevelt of Dakota Territory, "every wind bending the blades into a ripple, flecking the prairie with shifting patches of a different green . . . exactly as . . . a light squall or wind-gust will fleck the smooth surface of the ocean." It was not, however, these magnificent grasslands that first brought the young Theodore Roosevelt to Dakota in the 1880s.

It was buffalo, or, more correctly, *Bison bison*. He came to hunt bison in the autumn of 1883, even as the species—once reckoned at 60 million animals—was heading to the brink of extinction and, ironically, also becoming the very symbol of the American West. In the previous few decades the bison, which had roamed in endless dark waves across the plains, had been nearly exterminated by wanton slaughter. Roosevelt's rush to hunt one of a dying breed seems strange in the light of today's attitudes about conserving species. He was a product of his times; but he eventually became a promoter of conservation and, as honorary president of the American Bison Society, of the push to protect the remnant herd of bison—perhaps in part because of his experiences in Dakota. He had fallen in love with the region. Even the eroded badlands terrain that abuts the prairie had for him "a fantastic beauty of its own."

It was fitting, then, that here in the North Dakota badlands in 1947 the Theodore Roosevelt National Memorial Park be dedicated to honor our 26th President—urbane New Yorker though he was. Teddy's story is still inextricably linked with the park. When, in 1978, the 70,447-acre reserve achieved full national park status, it was renamed simply Theodore Roosevelt National Park.

Roosevelt had to travel far to find his buffalo. And once in Dakota Territory, he spent ten grueling days tracking the coveted prize.

Dark-eyed sunflowers bob in a summer breeze. Multitudes of wildflowers add rich color to windswept prairie grasslands.

PRECEDING PAGES: Riders ford the Little Missouri River in North Dakota's Theodore Roosevelt National Park. The park preserves rare prairie and badlands terrain as well as honoring the 26th U. S. President.

THEODORE ROOSEVELT NATIONAL PARK

LOCATION: North Dakota
ESTABLISHED: November 10, 1978
SIZE: 70,416 acres

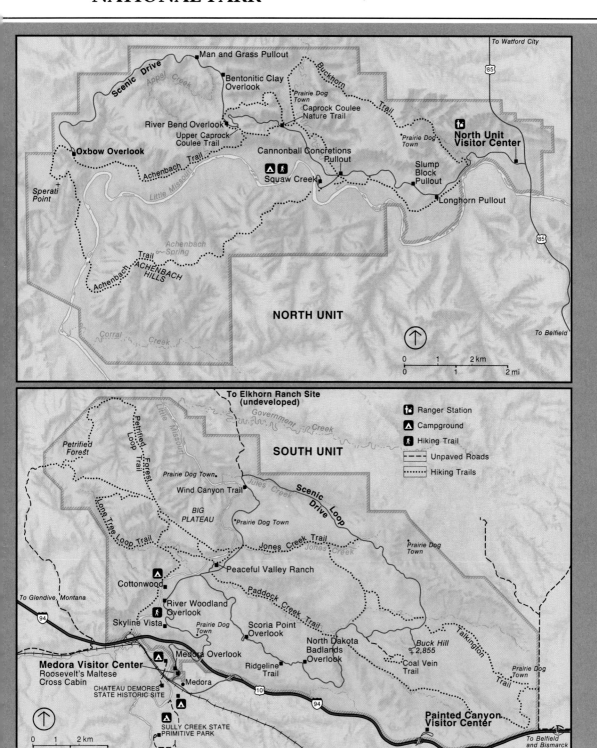

NORTH UNIT

To Watford City

Man and Grass Pullout
Scenic Drive
Appel Creek
Bentonitic Clay Overlook
Buckhorn Trail
Prairie Dog Town
Caprock Coulee Nature Trail
River Bend Overlook
Upper Caprock Coulee Trail
Achenbach Trail
Cannonball Concretions Pullout
Squaw Creek
Prairie Dog Town
North Unit Visitor Center
Slump Block Pullout
Longhorn Pullout
Oxbow Overlook
Little Missouri
Sperati Point
Achenbach Spring
Achenbach Trail
ACHENBACH HILLS
Corral Creek

85
85

To Belfield

0   1   2 km
0   1   2 mi

SOUTH UNIT

To Elkhorn Ranch Site (undeveloped)
Little Missouri
Government Creek
Petrified Forest Loop Trail
Petrified Forest
Prairie Dog Town
Jules Creek
Wind Canyon Trail
Scenic Loop Drive
BIG PLATEAU
Long Tree Loop Trail
Prairie Dog Town
Jones Creek Trail
Jones Creek
Prairie Dog Town
Peaceful Valley Ranch
Cottonwood
Paddock Creek Trail
To Glendive, Montana
River Woodland Overlook
Skyline Vista
Prairie Dog Town
Scoria Point Overlook
North Dakota Badlands Overlook
Buck Hill 2,855
Talkington Trail
Prairie Dog Town
94
Medora Overlook
Ridgeline Trail
Coal Vein Trail
Medora Visitor Center
Roosevelt's Maltese Cross Cabin
Medora
CHATEAU DEMORES STATE HISTORIC SITE
10
94
Painted Canyon Visitor Center
SULLY CREEK STATE PRIMITIVE PARK
To Belfield and Bismarck

0   1   2 km
0   1   2 mi

Ranger Station
Campground
Hiking Trail
Unpaved Roads
Hiking Trails

For days at a time he lived happily on biscuits and rainwater. He greeted icy rain and deprivations with such cheerful exclamations as "By Godfrey, but this is fun!"

Successful in finally bringing down a bison bull, Roosevelt celebrated with an Indian war dance, then headed back to New York. Eight months later, he was back in Dakota Territory to take up cattle ranching. Never robust as a young man, he now boasted of "working as hard as any of the cowboys. . . . Yesterday I was eighteen hours in the saddle—from 4 a.m. to 10 p.m. . . . I can now do cowboy work pretty well." He gained strength in body and character, and learned, he said, "to measure men right." He asserted later, too, that were it not for his time in Dakota, he would not have become President.

*R*EMOTENESS KEEPS Theodore Roosevelt among the lesser known national parks. And, perhaps, its northern clime. "The wind blows so much here," one person told me, "that in winter when it stops snowing, we don't know it for about three days!" Though the park is located at the edge of an interstate, the highway is not heavily traveled. A lot of people don't stop at the park. "Most," one observer said, "are passing through on their way to somewhere else—the general fate of all of North Dakota."

Just off the interstate coming from the east, high on the escarpment at the Painted Canyon rest area, you get a first glimpse into the park. A colorful, crumbling badlands terrain yawns below at the edge of the prairie. Travelers enjoy what must be one of the most spectacular rest stops anywhere. For many visitors it is their only experience of the park. It's not enough.

The park deserves more time. Time to sit awhile and hear the quietness, feel the emptiness—to have a sense of what attracted Roosevelt to this remote region. Time to linger on a grassy knoll at sunset and wait for a mule deer or whitetail or elk to browse by. Or simply to watch the fading light draw a new veil across the scene with every passing minute—then to welcome the moon, the stars, and perhaps the northern lights streaking the inky prairie sky. Time to inhale the scent of sagebrush after a thunderstorm and watch, on the far horizon, a wild stallion round up his harem. And all the while to listen to the eerie serenade of coyotes from butte to butte.

The prairie grasses shimmered golden in the afternoon sun as I arrived in the wilds of western North Dakota and took a swing around the 36-mile loop road in the southern sector of the park. Plentiful spring rains had broken a drought of several years. Lush growth softened harsh badlands in velvety striations of green.

Divided into three distinct parts, Theodore Roosevelt park encompasses 218 acres of Roosevelt's original Elkhorn "home ranch," as well as large sections of badlands, strung out along the Little Missouri River as it wends northward to meet the Missouri. The South Unit snugs up against the fancifully rebuilt tourist village of Medora, near where TR had alighted from the train in 1883 to begin his western sojourn. Downriver 35 miles lies the small portion consisting of the Elkhorn. Still farther north along the river lies the more rugged and isolated North Unit where, as far as anyone knows, Roosevelt made only one foray. That was late one March, when he and his hands took off from the Elkhorn in hot pursuit of three men who had stolen his boat. He eventually arrested the malefactors and transported them by ice-choked river and overland to the town of Dickinson to face the law. The trip—lasting 13 days and covering 200 miles—was punishment enough, perhaps.

In recent years the park has focused as much on natural history and wilderness resources as on the original Roosevelt theme. As was the case with TR, though, bison still bring people here. The possibility of an encounter with these wild animals adds to the park experience. "Dangerous if provoked," park literature warns. "They can run up to 35 miles per hour . . . turn faster than a horse. Please view them at a distance."

*U*NLIKE TEDDY, I had no trouble finding bison. Sometimes, in fact, it was more of a problem to avoid them, along park trails especially. Bison are smart animals; they pick the best routes through this badlands terrain, and human trails follow them. Wide bison paths often crisscross park trails. It's easy to take the wrong path and stray. "That's why we have to put up signposts," a ranger explained, "even in wilderness areas. But even that doesn't always do any good—the bison use them for scratching posts and knock them down."

Once a lone bull, handsome and prime, came along a narrow trail I was on. He snorted and wheeled out of sight but then recovered his composure and continued toward me. Now it was I who leapt out of the way, down a hillside. Another time, two hiking companions and I scrambled up some fragile sandstone formations to avoid ten bison that suddenly appeared around a bend in a trail. Even when I wasn't seeing bison, I found signs of them: teeth; horns; a tuft of coarse hair caught on a tree branch; a juniper trunk rubbed to a polish by scratching; large, flat footprints; dusty depressions where bison wallow; scat, humorously known in the region as "prairie pizzas."

After TR's time the wild bison disappeared from their prairie habitat. These animals in the park were reintroduced—as were the pronghorn and the elk. And they have flourished. It is, after all, their natural habitat. The park has also reestablished a few Longhorn cattle.

John Heiser remembers vividly the day in 1962 when the buffalo came back to the North Unit. (They were already back in the South Unit by 1956.) "I will never forget. It was a main event, so we all came down. And they turned them loose in the North Unit, right on the sagebrush flat where the Longhorn pullout is—20-some head!" Third-generation rancher, park ranger, and dedicated environmentalist— a combination unusual in this region of ranchers and farmers—John was showing me around the North Unit, where he works. "Buffalo are incredible animals," he said. "They are the essence of the plains."

Even so, this is not a truly wild herd, nor can it ever be. The problem with the bison in the park now is one of management. The old predators, the grizzly and the wolf, are long gone. The bison can no longer follow their natural migration routes and thus avoid overgrazing their range. Regular roundups and stout fences must now keep the bison in and their number at around 400 or 500.

Despite precautions, bison do occasionally escape the confines of the park. It does not make nearby ranchers happy, though generally relations between ranchers and the park are good.

"We bought a prize bull a couple of years ago," Bruce Kaye, the park's chief naturalist, told me, explaining how the park handles owners' grievances. "A bison bull had rendered it useless!"

We were on our way to see the Elkhorn site. The road was getting rougher. "People are always amazed that Roosevelt could take his buckboard out here," said Bruce. "He had to cross the river maybe 17 times!" Little remains of the large log house at the site except maybe a couple of cornerstones, now almost lost in tall grass, and the cottonwoods—old and contorted, with branches broken or dead—that stood beside the long-gone veranda. It's a kind of pilgrimage to come here now. To pass the time with TR in the "hot noontide hours of midsummer...," listening "to the cottonwood trees overhead, whose shimmering, tremulous leaves ... rustle and quaver and sigh all day long." What was it about these Dakota grasslands that lured such aristocratic dudes as TR and the Marquis de Mores, an eccentric young French nobleman? They were trading the narrow constraints of civilized society for adventure in the romantic West. They came expensively accoutered—TR with silver spurs, alligator boots, and a hunting knife from Tiffany's. They wanted to make money, too, inspired by the glowing promises offered by such contemporary best-sellers as James S. Brisbin's *Beef Bonanza; or, How to Get Rich on the Plains.*

The Marquis de Mores arrived first, early in 1883, stepping off the train at a rough collection of shacks called Little Missouri—"Little Misery" to the locals. Just across the river he founded the town of Medora, naming it after his wife. The large frame farmhouse he built became known as the Château de Mores. His life-style, complete with servants, flowing champagne, and ten-course meals, bestowed an aura of European nobility upon the town. People came out to watch the endless parade of trunks containing Medora's wardrobe being unloaded from the train. The Marquis de Mores's commercial establishment was less glamorous: a large abattoir that prepared dressed beef for shipment east in refrigerated railroad cars.

The chief reminders of the de Mores's life in Medora are a brick chimney from the abattoir and the château, now a museum. Not much survives either of Roosevelt and the short-lived era of open-range ranching, which perished with the cattle in the terrible winter of 1886-87. But permanent settlers arrived to ranch and farm after those adventurous times in the 1880s. And TR lived in the mind of at least one of them, Ted Cornell. He didn't know Roosevelt himself, but his father did, and his grandfather.

*T*HEN IN HIS 70s, Ted had been Billings County sheriff for 30 years. For decades, too, he had taken care of the Medora cemetery, atop a hill above town. Strangely enough it was among those gravestones one morning, in the easy laugh of Ted Cornell and in his stories, that old Medora came most to life for me. "Reason I got so tall is that I stayed green a long time!" said Ted, who was a big man. He credited his 6-foot-6-inch stature for his effectiveness as sheriff. "Sometimes all I had to do was stand up! As sheriff I never drew a gun on any man, though I've been shot at. It was a lot wilder in Medora when I was young. People would get drunk and ride their horses into the bars and holler and scream."

Ted came by his storytelling rightly. His grandfather, Norman Lebo, who is buried here, was a talker too. He was Roosevelt's cook for a while. "TR was supposed to have said," Ted confessed with a laugh, "that my grandfather had the 'biggest library of miscellaneous misinformation' of any man he knew. But he didn't call him a god-damned liar. So I've tried to carry on!"

We meandered among the gravestones, and Ted regaled me with tales of the settlers who peopled Billings County: Riley Luffsey—for whose murder de Mores was tried and acquitted—lies here, as well as an assortment of trappers, cowboys, Civil War veterans, and some dead about whom little is known, such as the person beneath the headstone mysteriously inscribed, "The Man The Bank Fell On."

Judging from the cemetery, it must have been a motley crew that came here to settle, but the rangeland gave them good value. "The grass here has a lot of strength," a rancher told me in Medora. "It cures in the fall; it dries out before it freezes, as a rule, and holds its strength, its food value."

Some of that original prairie is preserved in the park. "The thing that's nice," said Myron Freeman, "is that these are all native plants here. It's just like the native environment you might have seen 100 or 200 years ago." I joined Professor Freeman, then a naturalist at Dickinson State University, for a walk along the Ridgeline Trail in the South Unit. From atop the ridge we looked out over a breathtaking vista of prairie and badlands. To an uneducated eye the grasses that rippled like silk in the breeze all looked the same. But it is the intricate ecology, Myron explained, the rich variety that makes for good grazing. Different plants give sustenance at different times of the year. The two most typical shortgrass prairie species, the buffalo and the blue grama, are summer grasses.

"This is male buffalo grass," Myron said, pointing to some insignificant-looking little spikes two or three inches high. "The female plants spread along the ground like crabgrass." Myron picked up some threadleaf sedge. "It comes early in the springtime. This isn't even grass. See the triangular stems, instead of round. Bison eat that. Deer, too." Some plants provide salt. Others, such as a sage look-alike called winter fat, provide forage for browsers when little else is available. Even plants the animals don't eat, such as sagebrush, have an important role. "Some ranchers got rid of the sagebrush. Used sprays. Thought they'd have more food for their livestock." But they didn't succeed in growing more grass. In fact, the sage had helped capture snow, adding moisture to the soil, and had also kept down erosion.

Blue-green, berry-laden female junipers and bright green male ones grow thick on the north-facing slopes. Hardwoods and cottonwoods flourish lower down. Vegetation serves as a compass. "You look south and everything is vegetated," Myron said. "You look northward and very little grows. You never can get lost here."

I'm not so sure. I think it would be easy to get lost in the badlands. It's a surreal, malleable environment—like a scene in a Salvador Dali painting, a world melting away. Ridges and plateaus slump into layer cakes, dribbling icings of stone. Sandstone formations, waterpocked, succumb gradually like giant sandcastles to invisible tides. Rivulets of stone drape pillars, capped by harder, more resistant strata. If you squint a little, buttes soften into pyramids and fortressed cities.

For the creation of this landscape the Rocky Mountains can take some credit. Fire and ice have had a role, too. More recently, water—river and rain—has taken charge. Some 60 million years ago, when the Rockies were being uplifted, rivers ran swiftly eastward, dumping eroded material onto a broad alluvial plain that once covered this area. Layer upon layer of sedimentary rock built up. Volcanic ash, blasted from the western mountains, added layers that became slick, gray bentonite clay. Era followed era, warm, moist, and forested sometimes, then desert again. Depending on conditions, forests were fossilized or were transformed into lignite coal beds. That's what brings fire into the story. *(Continued on page 82)*

ERWIN & PEGGY BAUER

*S*pring greens a
rumpled landscape at
Painted Canyon. Despite
eroded topography, these
badlands support wildlife
and livestock with a wide
range of plants. Junipers
and other brush on north-
facing slopes retain scarce
moisture and provide
shelter. Raptors such as this
prairie falcon (top) find
plentiful prey in the park.
Jagged sandstone
formations (above) near
Wind Canyon rise above
layers of gray bentonite in
the foreground—described
by Theodore Roosevelt as
" 'gumbo' clay which rain
turns into slippery glue."

Relics of Dakota dudes: The Maltese Cross Cabin (below) sheltered TR early in his Dakota sojourn, before he moved north to Elkhorn Ranch. Restored now at park headquarters, the log cabin once stood seven miles to the south.

Teddy look-alike, Mark Klemetsrud re-creates TR and his hearty style for visitors. The Maltese Cross branding iron he holds marked steers at TR's first ranch. Frenchman Marquis de Mores and his wife, Medora, lived in the capacious farmhouse opposite. Hired hands took meals in this kitchen at the "Château de Mores," while the family ate in the formal dining room off Medora's 500-piece set of English Minton china.

*H*ome again on the range, bison graze spring's
lush growth in Theodore Roosevelt park. All but vanished in
Roosevelt's time and replaced by cattle, bison have flourished
since their reintroduction into the park in 1956. A prairie dog
scans its territory for predators, its view improved by bison
trimming the grass. Wild horses—some, legend says, descended
from those of Sitting Bull—also have multiplied here. The park
must cull all large grazers from time to time.

"Hell with the fires out," was how Gen. Alfred Sully, who skirmished with the Sioux near here in 1864, characterized these broken, eroded badlands. He had the right idea. But the fires are not quite out yet. A couple of years before my visit a bed of lignite in a remote part of the South Unit had caught fire, ignited perhaps by lightning or a range fire. Bruce Kaye and I set out to see if it was still burning. We traced a lignite bed along a slope. A mountain bluebird flashed by, the bluest bird I'd ever seen. Gangly masses of sunflowers bloomed bright at the feet of ghostly, charred tree trunks.

"This whole ridge of trees burned right off. The sunflowers are the pioneer species," said Bruce. He and other park staff had come out to contain the fire. Another such fire, near the Coal Vein Trail on the other side of the park, burned from 1951 until 1977, Bruce told me. "When that coal was burning there, people used to come out and roast marshmallows!"

Layers and outcroppings of bright red rock offer striking contrast to more neutral strata. "It's called scoria around here, though strictly speaking it's not really scoria, which is volcanic in origin," said Bruce. Layers of clay above the burning lignite are baked into a brick-like substance. The red color comes with the release of iron oxide. The odor of sulfur and coal still permeated the air. A wisp of smoke wafted upward. Bruce put his hand into one crevice and quickly snatched it out. The fire was still burning. I tested the crumbling, dark substance—it was like putting my hand in the hot ashes of a fireplace.

*I*N MORE RECENT TIMES, geologically speaking, ice comes into the story, influencing the shaping of sediments laid down by the western rivers—and the final formation of the badlands. From the Oxbow Overlook in the North Unit you can see clearly what happened.

"The glaciers came right to here," David Kuehn explained. Far below we could see the Little Missouri, flowing in sweeping curves, then making an abrupt U-turn. "Before the glacial period the river flowed north toward Hudson Bay. Then glaciers blocked the way. The river was forced south and eastward. But then the slope was steeper, and the river began to downcut swiftly through the sedimentary layers, exposing them and shaping the terrain we now see. It's still going on—with every rainstorm or high water on the river." By making calculations of sediment load in the river, some scientists estimate that the badlands are disappearing at a rate of five inches a year.

From David, an archaeologist from Texas A & M University who has surveyed many sites in the park, I learned something else about the badlands. The Sioux name for this tortuous terrain was *Mako Shika*, "land bad," and French explorers called it *les mauvaises terres à traverser*—"bad lands to cross." But for many people and animals these lands were extremely *good* lands. For a long time it was thought that prehistoric Native Americans avoided the region or merely passed through on their way to somewhere else. But recent archaeological surveys by David and others have come up with a different conclusion. "We've found projectile points dating back through the last 10,000 years. The early theory that archaic people just passed through here is, I feel through my research, a gross simplification."

Erosion may be the reason that so little evidence has remained of the early inhabitants. Any artifacts or other traces on the floodplain would have been carried away. "But erosion is also the reason why this badlands area was desirable," David contends. "Flora and fauna were limited on the rolling plains. The badlands relief provided a whole lot of different ecotones—niches—for plants and animals. North-facing slopes support trees that offered year-round cover for elk, deer, and bighorn sheep, and winter shelter for buffalo." Erosion cut into the aquifers, exposing water. He pointed to a high bluff. "That blocked the northwesterly winds that prevail here in winter. The badlands were *very* attractive to prehistoric people."

We wandered across a prairie dog town where David had been working. Two groups of prehistoric people wintered here, he thinks, one about 5,000 to 3,000 years ago and another about 2,000 years ago. But now the prairie dogs were in residence, and they popped up from their burrows like jack-in-the-boxes. The rotund little rodents berated us fiercely with high-pitched yipping—they were dubbed *petits chiens,* "little dogs," by French explorers. They dig up artifacts, David told me.

Every now and then, where I saw nothing, he stooped to pick up a bone or a piece of Knife River flint from an area east of here. "This is a side scraper," he said. The people probably stayed here three or four months and pursued a range of activities with impressive efficiency. "They would use everything from the bison they hunted," David said. "Even the bones they pulverized and rendered by boiling into bone grease, a lardlike staple that lasted indefinitely."

One evening I set out on horseback from Peaceful Valley Ranch with some friends for an overnight trip. We headed northward, crossing the river, then cut across the bottomland and picked our way carefully through the close-clipped, pungent expanse of a prairie dog town. "This is the supermarket of the prairie," said Wally Owen, a local rancher who operates Peaceful Valley Ranch, the trail-ride concession in the park. Though their main predator of the past, the black-footed ferret, is gone from the park and now endangered, prairie dogs are not free of enemies. Plenty of other creatures still prey on them: coyotes, snakes, eagles, and badgers. Snakes and owls evict them from their burrows. A gray bird flew by close to the ground. "A burrowing owl," said Wally. "They nest in prairie dog burrows." And if that's not enough, bison find the bare mound entrances to the burrows irresistible places for wallowing. Surprisingly enough, however, bison and prairie dogs have a symbiotic relationship. Bison grazing keeps the vegetation short for the little dogs, providing them with clear visibility to detect predators, and bison wallowing leaves depressions that catch water and encourage new plant growth—forage for both species.

We left the bottomland and started a long climb up grassy slopes. Golden light faded fast into blue, with a rising moon. Four elk bulls emerged from some brush and climbed toward the ridge. On the crest they paused a second, silhouetted against the bright twilight sky, then dropped out of sight. We bedded down under big canvas tents, lulled by crooning coyotes—"song dogs" to the Indians—and deer munching close to the tent wall.

AT DAWN MEADOWLARKS sang out reveille. We moved at a leisurely pace back toward the ranch. Or so we thought. Just beyond the prairie dog town, an old bison bull suddenly stood up and shook the dust off himself as if to announce his presence and, it turned out, that of 60 or 70 of his fellows. They had spread out in the night over the bottomland by the river. There was no way to ride horses through the herd. The bison were popping up everywhere. Our guide decided that we should head up a draw behind the herd, then climb the high ridges and drop down behind them. That was the plan.

We would soon learn the true meaning of mauvaises terres à traverser. It was a lesson Teddy Roosevelt had learned before us. "In much of the Bad Lands," he wrote, "it needs genuine mountaineer skill to get through . . . and no horse but a Western one, bred to the business, could accomplish the feat."

Well, we had the Western horses. And they headed easily up one grassy, juniper-dotted north-facing slope. The soil held firm. Over the top of the ridge we saw vividly illustrated the difference between a north- and south-facing slope. A crumbling, arid, eroded southward slope dropped off in front of us. The horses picked their way across a narrow game trail, then dropped down into a gully. Cody, the mare I rode, balked a little, but she was merely taking stock of the situation. She soon picked her route and slid down the steep drop partly on her expansive rump. The ridges beyond offered the same story. Lush north-facing slopes offered good footing, but beyond the ridge came the treacherously eroded southward face. Finally one ridge presented no possible route. By the time we circled back to the bottomland, most of the bison had moved along. We made it home to the ranch an hour or so late—and intimately acquainted with badlands terrain. I had acquired in the process boundless respect for the cowboys who chase cows in this convoluted country.

To an extent its isolation protects Theodore Roosevelt. But even here there are threats. Such invasive exotics as leafy spurge—which may degrade the quality of the rangeland—bother park superintendent Pete Hart. Something else bothers him more: development just outside park boundaries. "We are trying to protect the sense of isolation that Teddy Roosevelt would have experienced," Hart pointed out, "particularly at the Elkhorn." The problem is that in recent years oil has been discovered. Theodore Roosevelt National Park lies atop part of a major oil and gas reserve.

"We can't just say we are against energy development," said Hart. "I drive a car. You drove a car here. Everybody who works here drives a car." The impact of the oil wells is already apparent. At the Elkhorn Ranch site you can hear the pop-pop-pop of the pump generator and see the gas flares above the butte across the Little Missouri. And something like 500 more wells are planned for the surrounding region—some very close to the park.

Pete Hart was positive, as I left him, that compromises can be worked out with oil developers. And he hopes more people will discover the park. "You can see more wildlife here in an hour and a half than in a whole day in Yellowstone," he boasts. "I think this is probably one of the best kept secrets in the entire National Park System."

Just before leaving, I walked with Bruce Kaye across the Big Plateau area of the park. From a distance we could hear a low sound reverberating almost like thunder—half snort, half rumble. Leonine. We came up over a grassy rise and found ourselves almost on top of a large group of bison that had gathered for the rutting season. Four or five adolescent bulls chased each other up and down in a line. Calves fed, nuzzled their mothers, and cavorted. Bulls, magnificent in their dark woolliness, inspected cows for readiness to mate.

With the wind behind us, they were beginning to notice us too, casting baleful looks our way. The prickly-pear-filled depression Bruce and I had picked out on the treeless prairie for a quick retreat, should it be required, looked less and less adequate.

Still, the bulls seemed more interested in their companions than in us, and we retreated quietly along the grassy hillside. Once the whole prairie must have been like this. The deep, resonant rumbling of the bison now became fainter. A sound like no other. Can you imagine how 60 million of them would have sounded?

FOLLOWING PAGES: Storm sky bends to the prairie. The park gives a sense of Dakota grasslands that TR described as "one gigantic, unbroken pasture, where cowboys and branding-irons take the place of fences."

Weathered timbers of a homesteader's dwelling
(above) succumb to age—and bring to mind the hardy breed
that settled these rugged lands. The visitors shown here brought
their own horses to explore this remote corner of the North
Unit's Achenbach Hills. Under a ranger's tutelage, a smaller
visitor pursues serious study of native prairie coneflowers.
Throughout the park, the western meadowlark, called by TR
"one of the sweetest and most incessant singers we have,"
breaks the quiet in "a rich, strong voice."

Lazy meanderings of the Little Missouri belie the river's power. Dammed here at the North Unit's Oxbow by glaciers during the Ice Age, the river turned southward onto a steeper gradient. The stream then carved more rapidly through the layers of sediment, helping

to create the tumbled terrain of today. Badlands have long attracted wildlife to their abundant variety of foods. Cattle, such as the Longhorn opposite, were driven here by cowboys in the 1880s. A small herd in the park recalls those adventuresome days of open-range ranching.

Channel Islands
A Park Apart

By Tom Melham
Photographs by James A. Sugar and Norbert Wu

*I*T IS NOT your typical national park. For starters, you can't drive there from here; it's part of an archipelago off southern California. Would-be visitors must book passage by boat or small plane, neither of which comes cheap when you're with family. But look on the bright side: Imagine a national park without Winnebagos.

Imagine a California of another century, with mile after mile of shoreline absolutely untouched by freeways, the surfing scene, or mission-style developments. Imagine an American Galápagos, where a unique collection of wildlife varies from island to island. Imagine also a former Navy bombing range, a working cattle ranch, rugged coasts littered with ghostly shipwrecks, and lively "forests" of giant kelp. Imagine Channel Islands National Park.

It is barely 17 years old, and it is a park of human manufacture, undergoing long-term rehabilitation from past exploitation and oversight, in the same way a derelict old mansion can be made to glow anew.

"It's the wave of the future," says Superintendent C. Mack Shaver. "Any land the Park Service acquires now is going to need this kind of treatment, because wilderness just isn't available any more. Everything's been altered. Pristine? We got the last of that with the Alaska parks. There's *nothing* left in the lower 48."

Mack's present bailiwick includes five of California's eight Channel Islands—so called because they flank the Santa Barbara Channel just north of Los Angeles. The five are: San Miguel, Santa Rosa, Santa Cruz, Anacapa—the four northern Channel Islands—and Santa Barbara island, lone park representative from the southern group. Together, Santa Barbara and Anacapa composed the park's precursor, Channel Islands National Monument, created in 1938 by President

Sedentary but deadly, a white-spotted rose anemone uses stinging tentacles to overpower mobile prey such as this bat star.

PRECEDING PAGES: Rocky serpent of Anacapa—one of five isles forming Channel Islands National Park—snakes across the park's namesake waterway, southern California's Santa Barbara Channel.

NORBERT WU (OPPOSITE); JEFF GNASS (PRECEDING PAGES)

Franklin Roosevelt. Both are small, rocky affairs, best known for their important seabird rookeries and scuba diving opportunities.

Anacapa lies nearest the mainland, a mere 11 miles southwest of Oxnard. It is long and narrow, fragmented into three main islets and smaller offshore rocks that, like sea serpents gracing old maps, break the ocean in a dotted line of curving humps. Its name means "mirage" or "ever changing" in the language of coast-dwelling Chumash Indians, who had lived here many centuries by the time Spanish explorers first saw them in 1542. The Chumash were a peaceful lot, subsisting largely off the sea while roaming tidal areas and the channel in seagoing canoes. Today, Island Packers—the park concessionaire—will boat you here in a sleek cabin cruiser for $45 each ($25 for kids); passengers may disembark to hike island trails, picnic, or take in the lighthouse that now caps one islet. Many visitors, however, come less for the land than for the sea, whose riches beckon scuba divers.

In most of the park, too, both sport and commercial fishing are legal. No matter that the park itself extends a nautical mile out from shore; no matter that the surrounding national marine sanctuary extends for six nautical miles; this "sanctuary" is a shadow, protecting seafloor but not inhabitants. Its basic purpose is to keep offshore oil platforms—which already dot Santa Barbara Channel—from nudging nearer the islands. In or out of park and sanctuary, the taking of abalone or tuna or giant kelp or any other species is regulated not by federal bureaucracies but by the California Fish and Game Department.

SLIPPING BENEATH THE WAVES off Anacapa, I dropped about 50 feet through plankton-clouded waters to a sand bottom that first seemed sterile but soon gave way to crags sprouting a wealth of life. Thumb-size holdfasts of giant kelp clung to the rock, giving rise to braided stalks and flat, leaflike blades that reached all the way to the water's surface, forming there a vast canopy continually in motion with the sea. These huge algae shelter all sorts of life along their branched and crannied surfaces: Tiny, shrimp-like isopods hold as firmly to the stalks as scales on a snake; little fish try to hide from big fish; grazers and predators alike seek meals in the varied communities that thrive in and around the kelp. On the rocky floor, sea urchins lay in clefts, idly twitching their spines, and giant keyhole limpets resembled staring, disembodied eyes. A large sea hare—a shell-less mollusk with rabbitlike "ears"—munched on algae encrusting a boulder. Kelp bass and rockfish flitted about, as tiny Catalina gobies—red, with narrow bands of electric blue—sparkled atop drab rocks fringed with colorful feather duster worms.

I left the kelp bed for more open waters and suddenly found myself encased in a slow-moving vortex of silvery streaks. Thousands

CHANNEL ISLANDS NATIONAL PARK

LOCATION: California
ESTABLISHED: March 5, 1980
SIZE: 248,515 acres

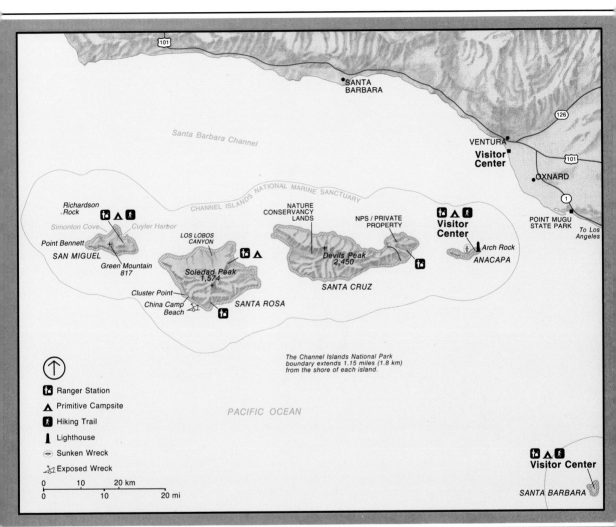

of anchovies encircled me not an arm's length away, half of them lei-surely curving around clockwise and half in the opposite direction, just outside the others. Their gleaming bodies moved and meshed with such coordination they seemed part of some greater organism.

Low on air, I broke from the entrancing anchovies and headed back toward the boat. A grim deltoid shape, like a Stealth Bomber with a two-foot wingspan, sped by: a bat ray! Six or eight more followed in formation, trailing long needle tails; then a second squadron zoomed past. Perhaps because they swim in straight lines, undulating vertically rather than side-to-side like most fish, bat rays always seem bent on some purpose. They are dark, silent types; some people find their bul-bous heads and raised, octopus eyes sinister. They smack of mystery, of another world. One condescendingly let me tail it for a moment, then tired of the game and darted silently off.

Westward from Anacapa lies Santa Cruz, the largest, tallest, most varied, and most liveable of the Channel Islands. Nine-tenths of its 62,000 acres belong to The Nature Conservancy, which purchased the tract in 1978 before the park was formed. It serves as a Conservancy showpiece, often used for entertaining donors, executives, and other VIPs who come to learn about Santa Cruz and the Conservancy's preservation work. With its mid-19th-century buildings—made of brick from local clay—its citrus-and-avocado orchards, its flower gardens exploding in color, and its swimming pool, the main ranch on Santa Cruz stands out as a shady retreat amid ravined and sunbaked mountains. Towering, century-old eucalyptus trees line the approaches. It all seems a world away from southern California's freeway frenzy.

Conservancy program director Jim Sulentich explained why: "Seventeen million people live within a hundred-mile radius of this place. Logistics keep it protected. If it were part of the mainland, there'd be wall-to-wall people. What better depicts a nature preserve in a turbulent world than an island in the middle of an ocean?"

WELL, NOT QUITE THE MIDDLE: Santa Cruz lies only 21 miles from the continent. And it seems terribly civilized for a "nature preserve." Past owners here lived like barons. Once a Mexican land grant, Santa Cruz was bought piecemeal over the 1870s and '80s by Justinian Caire, a French emigré who profited from the gold rush. He planted his island with grasses suitable for livestock, along with vineyards, orchards, and other crops, creating an independent and self-contained homestead. His winery, which produced some prizewinning vintages, still stands. So does a quaint chapel, renovated in 1991 for its 100th birthday.

Caire's family sold most of Santa Cruz to businessman Edwin L. Stanton in 1930, and Stanton's son Carey eventually inherited it. Carey Stanton grew to love the place deeply, becoming increasingly concerned over the years for its future; he had no heirs. He considered turning it over to the Park Service, but balked.

"Stanton just couldn't imagine this island turned into a public vacation spot," Jim told me. "When he asked the Conservancy if it would be interested in the island, we said, 'We don't know. Let's look.' We sent biologists—and they found 48 rare and endangered plants on Santa Cruz that don't occur on the mainland. Roughly 38 are shared with the other Channel Islands. That was incentive, because our mission is to preserve biological diversity. Santa Cruz isn't pristine. But it *is* the habitat of rare and endangered species."

Giving me a quick island tour by Landcruiser, Jim pointed out a couple of those special 48 species. "Here's Santa Cruz ironwood; it goes all the way to Nevada in the fossil record, but today it exists only on Santa Rosa and Santa Cruz." We left the shady central valley for drier uplands, passing chaparral aromatic with mountain lilac and bush poppy. Gullies gouged some areas, the result of past overgrazing. Despite a recent five-year drought that devastated island pines, dwarf "forests" of native oak survived, as did pastures of wild oat, an introduction. A kestrel, or "sparrow hawk," soared. Said Jim, "It's surprisingly diverse. Islands, especially those that have never been connected to a mainland, become populated by chance arrivals of plants and animals. We call it sweepstakes dispersal."

How did they get here? Birds and insects flew, or were blown over. Land animals either swam or rode rafts of floating debris. While the size, shape, and number of Channel Islands have varied with glaciation's changing sea levels—once forming a superisland geologists call Santarosae—no land bridge ever connected them to the rest of California. All life that reached these shores did so by crossing water.

Thus Santa Cruz's odd collection of native mammals: two predators, two rodents, and nine bats. In the Pleistocene epoch, perhaps as early as 40,000 years ago, mammoths also came to the islands, probably swimming from the mainland. They quickly evolved into a dwarf variety, presumably because of limited food resources.

"On islands, populations are so limited that funny characteristics tend to show up," Jim explained. "There are two island trends—gigantism and dwarfism. The island fox, like the mammoth, is a good example of the latter. Its closest mainland relative, the gray fox, is typically dog-size—while the island fox is more like a house cat."

But what of the scrub jay, a Santa Cruz endemic that's about 30 percent *larger* than its mainland counterpart? Or the "giant mouse," an upscale variety 10 percent bigger than the common deer mouse? Jim addressed the seeming contradiction: "Say you're a deer mouse. When you first get here, you're the only kind of mouse on the island. Back on the mainland you might have been one of six different species competing for food. Here, you get maybe 80 percent of the food choices you once had, but no one to fight with. So you start showing gigantism." A genetic predisposition to large size probably helps.

Because of the limitations and opportunities that islands present, Jim added, "everything that got out here was a player," including the domestic animals brought onto the island. When the Conservancy arrived on Santa Cruz in 1978, it found about 33,000 sheep severely overgrazing the land. It took nine years to kill them all—and then feral pigs proliferated on the carcasses. Far more resourceful and more destructive than sheep, the hogs have irked islanders for decades, and now the Conservancy is studying what to do about them. Cattle already have been reduced to a mere 13 head lorded over by Fred, a Longhorn bull whose rack, so the story goes, grew so wide he could no longer fit into the chutes used to load *(Continued on page 108)*

*M*iles *from any freeway, Anacapa's barren crags seasonally erupt in vivid yellow giant coreopsis— which in sheltered canyons may grow ten feet tall—and red prickly pear blossoms. Tour boats such as the* Jeffrey Arvid *(right) daily convey most visitors to park islands. On some trips, naturalists gather live residents from nearby shallows for a brief, hands-on, show-and-tell session aboard (below), then return the sea creatures to their homes.*

JAMES A. SUGAR / BLACK STAR (ABOVE AND BELOW)

*W*ild *facade of
Santa Cruz (left) contrasts
with a lush central valley,
where orchards and
outbuildings (top) recall
the island's glory days as a
private ranch. Today most
of Santa Cruz belongs to
The Nature Conservancy.
Part of the proceeds of
sales by mainland artists
such as Glenna Hartmann
goes to preservation.*

JOHN MACMURRAY JR.; FRANS LANTING / MINDEN PICTURES (BELOW)

Where sea meets Santa Rosa's rocky edge, death or life may triumph. Treacherous shoals, blinding fogs, and frequent gales cause numerous wrecks in the channel, a major shipping lane for Los Angeles. The freighter Chickasaw (below) broke up off Santa Rosa's southern coast in 1962. On shores such as China Camp Beach (opposite) lie quiet tidepools rich in shellfish and other marine creatures.

*H*ikers in grassy
*Los Lobos Canyon on
Santa Rosa (left) tread far
more lightly than the cattle
and sheep that once
severely overgrazed this
land. A permit system limits
visitor use; officials opened
some existing roads to
mountain bikers in 1992.
Prime Santa Rosa
attractions include
wildflowers and unique
local residents such as
diminutive island foxes
(above), which also inhabit
two other park islands.*

JC LEACOCK; LARRY ULRICH (RIGHT)

cattle boats bound for mainland slaughterhouses. Pragmatism won out over principle; the Conservancy let Fred remain, along with a harem of cows to insulate him from pangs of loneliness—and to serve as a living token of the island's long ranching history.

Ranching has dominated neighboring Santa Rosa, nearly as big as Santa Cruz but less varied, its repeating terrain as lumpy as buttermilk and concrete-hard. Few trees bless this island, and prolonged grazing has ravaged its pastures of introduced grasses. The former owners, who sold Santa Rosa to the Park Service in 1986, still ranch the island through a special-use permit good for up to 25 years. Sport hunting of Roosevelt elk and Kaibab deer was grandfathered in here as well. So although the island is now parkland with rangers in residence, you still can have a go at bagging an elk—that is, if you come up with the $6,000-to-$8,000 fee that guarantees a trophy head.

Preferring other quarry, I accompanied park archaeologist Don Morris on a search that took us to Cluster Point, on Santa Rosa's southwestern coast. Bare, gullied hills dropped off to dunes and beaches. Amid the dunes, a low rockpile partly covered in sand looked as unremarkable as a week-old campfire site. "That might be a Chumash sweat lodge," Don said. "It's prehistoric, probably—see how erosion is exposing it?" The Chumash, he explained, were a creative and active people, especially adept at exploiting marine resources with the *tomol,* a planked canoe of their own invention. Intimate knowledge of these shores enabled them to subsist here for thousands of years as they established extensive trading routes among island and mainland settlements.

On the beach we poked at scattered, partly buried timbers, one well over a foot square and perhaps 24 feet long. Bored holes and remnants of iron indicated nautical origins. Don thought it might be part of the *Dora Bluhm*—a wood-hulled lumber schooner, launched in 1883, that went down somewhere off this coast in 1910. She was one of scores of ships ranging from gold rush steamers to freighters and square-riggers that have come to grief in the Channel Islands over the centuries. Today, such wrecks increasingly draw sport divers as well as undersea archaeologists, Don said.

Minutes later, scrambling through pebbly, ravined foothills up from the beach, he spotted a mammoth femur sticking out from a gully like a flagpole from a wall. It was no less than 10,000 years old. We'd just seen probable evidence of prehistoric Indians, a 19th-century schooner, and now a Pleistocene mammoth—all within an hour. Little wonder Don likes Santa Rosa. "It's an archaeologist's paradise," he said. "I just flipped out when I first saw it. There's so much here, we still don't know what we have."

Neighboring San Miguel island, also rich in archaeological sites, is built to human scale—the sort of island you can walk across in a morning without feeling you're training for an Olympic event. It's isolated and somewhat desolate—as you'd expect for the outermost member of this chain, which bears the brunt of channel weather—but its terrain is pleasantly varied. Possessing neither Santa Cruz's craggy heights nor Santa Rosa's never-ending lumps, it consists more of sweeps: largely horizontal expanses of dunes, cliffs, hills, beaches. And unlike its two big sisters to the east, it never deludes you into believing you're anywhere but on an island; the sea's always in view.

Several Park Service paths lace San Miguel's surface and virtually rule out any chance of getting lost. Off-trail jaunts also are possible, ranger Mike Maki informed me. "But they're strictly with a guide. There are too many artifacts lying around. And unexploded shells. Most have been cleaned up, although in the two years I've been here I've come across three or four." Such relics recall the Navy's former use of the island as a bombing and missile range. Even now the Navy retains ownership, though the Park Service manages San Miguel.

"The other reason we don't want people wandering on their own," said Mike, "is the pinnipeds on the beaches. In the water, harbor seals are very curious and friendly. But hauled-out harbor seals —and sea lions—are real skittish." Human presence can spark a stampede, and pups always suffer in the crush. Tens of thousands of fur seals, sea lions, and elephant seals have made San Miguel *the* local rookery and breeding site. Before heading off to see them, I join Mike on a roundabout stroll to Simonton Cove.

*T*HE ISLAND'S CRANNIED BLUFFS wander, changing from tilted sediments to pebbly conglomerates to sand. Natural jetties segregate beaches and offshore shallows. But it is wildflowers that command the eye. Because this island spends most of the dry summer months under a blanket of fog, the ground stays moist; plants abound here, and something always seems to be in bloom. Mike, who with his naturalist wife, Mary Valentine, has identified some 80 different plant species on San Miguel, proves an able field guide. My questions on a purple-petaled whatnot, a red-flowered oddity, and a thick-leaved succulent are answered in rapid fire: "Seaside daisy. Island buckwheat. *Dudleya*—a type of stonecrop." Then there is the giant coreopsis, or tree sunflower, which stands three or four feet tall and erupts each spring with buttery yellow blossoms.

Much lower to the ground, magenta blooms of crystalline ice plants—an African import that has been taking over recently—look like land versions of sea anemones, their stems and leaves bejeweled with jelly blobs. Each blob is a sac that holds water. An ice plant concentrates salt from sea air. When it dies, the salt it releases so poisons the soil that nothing else can grow there—except another ice plant.

My arrival on San Miguel coincided with the Fourth of July weekend, the island's high season. No fewer than 22 pleasure boats crowded the lee shore of Cuyler Harbor, the island's best anchorage. Even so, nearby beaches bore no human footprints other than Mike's and my own. Before me stretched a ripply dune marked only by wind and a lone fox. Three fox kits played in the vegetation at dune's edge, exuberant as puppies. Seals and cormorants patrolled offshore shallows, while flotsam dappled the lower beach: timbers adrift from who-knew-where, scraps of kelp, weathered turban and abalone shells. With the boats at my back, Cuyler seemed solitude incarnate, a wild and untouched realm of sea, rock, and sand.

Next day, truly alone, I sampled San Miguel's main trail, which bisects the island east to west. Follow it, and if the wind is right, about the time you reach Green Mountain you'll hear what sounds like the distant wail of a hurricane, or perhaps the cyclical roar of surf. Continue, and this faint but unforgettable cry grows into a full-blown howler by trail's end at Point Bennett, a sandy polygon cornered in boulders that jut from the island's southwestern shore. Black and brown and gray dots rim the polygon: seals, sea lions, and elephant seals, perhaps 70 or 80 thousand all together. *They* are the source of the swirling, resonating wail. Male sea lions bellow loudest and longest, declaring territorial imperatives with a steady *ork-ork-ork* 24 hours a day.

"I don't really hear them any more," researcher Sharon Melin told me when I reached her station at Point Bennett. "Only if they stop—that's when I get up and look around."

SHARON, A BIOLOGIST with the National Marine Fisheries Service, studies local pinnipeds: California sea lions, northern fur seals, northern elephant seals, and harbor seals. All four species breed and pup here. "This is one of the world's largest breeding rookeries for California sea lions," said Sharon. "More than 70,000 come here during breeding season, giving birth to 18,000 or more pups yearly. One-third of *all* California sea lions are born here."

Like her boss, Robert Delong, who started this research program, Sharon finds all pinnipeds fascinating. Before us sprawls an incredible zoo of activity that compels human comparisons. This place could be Malibu: the beach clogged with sunbathers "hanging out," as scattered surfers ride the rollers, then drift out with the backwash and swim in for more. They may not be human, but what they do here can only be called play.

Sharon agrees: "Sea lions have such amiable personalities. On a hot day you'll see tons of young ones in the surf, porpoising through kelp beds, going up cliffs and jumping off, swimming around. They *do* play. Not in a human sense, perhaps, but they sure have lots of fun.

They love climbing on elephant seals. Sometimes you'll see two sea lion pups fighting on top of an elephant seal—and the seal just *sleeps.*"

Amid the sea of sea lions before us today roam a few thousand northern fur seals. They are the bullies of this beach, not kicking sand in faces but driving the more populous sea lions inland, away from desirable beachfront. Bands of northern elephant seals, recently returned from feeding forays to the Aleutian Islands, also show up. These huge, cigar-shaped slugs of blubber litter the sand like mindless cobbles. Most are motionless; signs of life are few and far between. Occasionally a foreflipper will stretch, curve, and deftly flick cool sand over the comatose body to which it's attached, only to fall motionless again.

A quantum leap in seal research came in 1990 with the development of "satellite packs"—lightweight, self-contained units that can be tracked anywhere on the globe via satellite. Affixed to seals with epoxy, they yielded startling revelations: for instance, that elephant seals trek twice yearly to the far north, where they gorge on squid—diving as deep as 5,000 feet for as long as 70 minutes at a time, over and over.

"It's amazing how deep they dive," says Sharon. "Nobody knew that before. Or that they migrate all the way to the Aleutians, then come all the way back to molt—and then *leave* again!" Molting, actually, is the major weakness of satellite packs, because they are attached to the animal's fur; as last year's coat falls off, so do they. Admits Sharon, "A lot of work still needs to be done."

I look again at this bleak sandspit that only a marine mammal could love and take in the nonstop cacophony, the incredible mass of life concentrated here. In a way, Point Bennett echoes the glorious profligacy of nature that was the Great Plains when numberless bison roamed there. It reaffirms the planet's awesome biological riches.

It was a thought echoed later by Mack Shaver, who told me: "In spite of fragmentation of ownership and diversity of use, the Channel Islands are relatively undisturbed. On the marine side—which is half the park—the ecosystems are unequalled anywhere in the contiguous U. S. The islands have been protected by their distance from the mainland. They've been likened to the Galápagos in the progression of biological changes that have taken place on them over thousands of years. Take the things that are out there—the unique species, both plants and animals. Take the cultural side, both recent history and Native American. Even the military history is unusual. Take all those things, and they make Channel Islands National Park really unique. There's no place else like it."

FOLLOWING PAGES: Crowds of California sea lions savor the sun and surf on San Miguel, the park's most remote island, home also to northern elephant seals and major seabird breeding colonies.

JAMES A. SUGAR / BLACK STAR

LARRY ULRICH (BOTH)

*S*noozing female elephant seal enjoys San Miguel's passive solar heating system (above), her flippers periodically flicking cool sand on her body to avoid overheating. Sand, rocks, sea, and near-total isolation from humans make the island's Point Bennett area (right) an ideal rookery for at least four pinniped species, which seasonally flock here in the tens of thousands.

In twilight even at midday, offshore forests of giant kelp (opposite) thrive near all Channel Islands, generating a wilderness atmosphere and a variety of marine life that draws sport divers. A bright-hued garibaldi (above)—California's state fish—picks an intruding sea urchin from its nest, a clearing it has made in hope of attracting a mate. A lone turban snail slowly grazes a kelp plant (left), eating not the kelp but tiny invertebrates living on it. Such denizens make kelp's colorful life web an enduring and unusual attraction of Channel Islands National Park.

Guadalupe Mountains
Desert Panorama

By Scott Thybony
Photographs by Michael Melford

C LIFFS DROPPED AWAY on three sides, disappearing into the early morning darkness below. Far to the east the arms of the old moon lifted above the horizon. Not long from now, the sun would follow. I had come to watch the sunrise from Guadalupe Peak, the highest point in Texas. Sitting on a sheltered ledge just beneath the summit, I was waiting until the last moment to face the winds on top. It was late spring in Guadalupe Mountains National Park, the tail end of a season when winds routinely reach hurricane force. "Strong enough to blow the wrinkles out of a dirt road," a rancher said.

Exaggeration comes naturally in this part of Texas west of the Pecos River. The region runs to extremes—high deserts and even higher mountains, little rain and even less flowing water. Its vast open spaces can be hypnotizing at highway speeds. But on foot in the sanctuary of the mountains, the sweep of the land loses its hold. The slow rhythm of walking unlocks the beauty of the Guadalupes.

The week before, I drove west across the scrub desert toward the national park, restless to head into new country. Dust, kicked up by the wind, scattered the morning sunlight. The mountains lay hidden behind the bright haze until I was 50 miles away; early travelers had reported seeing the range from 100 miles out on the plains. The uplands reach south from New Mexico, ending abruptly in a bold escarpment. Another scarp borders the far side of the mountains, out of view. These cliffs converge beneath the 8,749-foot summit of Guadalupe Peak in a dramatic promontory called El Capitan.

"Hour after hour we drove directly toward it," wrote explorer John Bartlett in the 1850s, "without seeming to approach nearer. . . ." He kept the landmark in sight for more than a week as he led a surveying party westward. Bartlett found the mountains increasingly dark

Solitary and free ranging, a mountain lion abandons its perch to roam the remote high country of the Guadalupes.

PRECEDING PAGES: First light strikes the scarred face of El Capitan, landmark promontory of Guadalupe Mountains National Park. More than half of this rugged desert park has been set aside as wilderness.

and gloomy as he neared what was known to be an Apache stronghold. Reaching the foot of the Guadalupes, he reported an attack on a wagon train there a few months before. Four men had lost their lives. Bartlett recorded the event matter-of-factly, but he didn't linger to enjoy the scenery.

More than a century later, the mountains no longer appeared threatening as I covered in an hour what Bartlett had taken days to cross. Near the park I pulled into the Nickel Creek Café for a hamburger and a cup of Mexican coffee. Two men sitting behind me talked casually about road conditions and the weather. The Mexican truck driver held up his end of the conversation in Spanish; the Texas rancher spoke English. They were careful not to mention the wind. Bad luck, I was told.

The next few days I spent talking with those who knew the mountains—geologists and park rangers, ranchers and Apache Indians. Finally I was ready to head for the high country.

The morning was unusually calm as I stood at the head of the trail leading into McKittrick Canyon. Under a hot sun I hoisted my pack with a groan. The lack of water in the backcountry meant carrying a gallon a day. Since my plan was to take three days crossing the park from east to west, that meant packing a lot of weight. I trudged up the trail under a load of sloshing water.

Scarcity of water had affected other forms of life besides backpackers. The trail began in classic Chihuahuan Desert country among plants with Tex-Mex names like lechuguilla, soaptree yucca, sotol. But the mouth of McKittrick Canyon offered few clues to what lay around the first bend.

I followed the trail across a dry creek bed paved with flood-tumbled cobbles. Soon the sparse desert vegetation retreated up the exposed slopes, and an unusual variety of trees crowded the canyon floor. The smooth, red bark of the Texas madrone felt so skinlike, it was hard to pass without a touch. The rough, checkered bark of an alligator juniper wasn't so tempting. Many of the species in McKittrick are living on the edge, having reached their geographical limits. The madrone rarely takes root farther north; the ponderosa pine

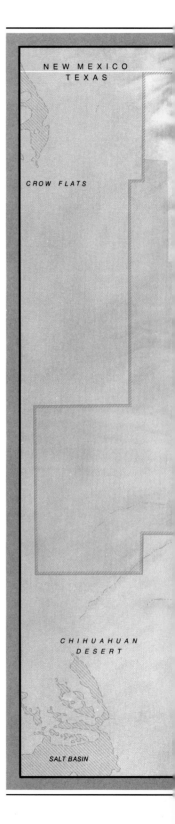

NEW MEXICO
TEXAS

CROW FLATS

CHIHUAHUAN
DESERT

SALT BASIN

GUADALUPE MOUNTAINS NATIONAL PARK

LOCATION: Texas
ESTABLISHED: September 30, 1972
SIZE: 86,416 acres

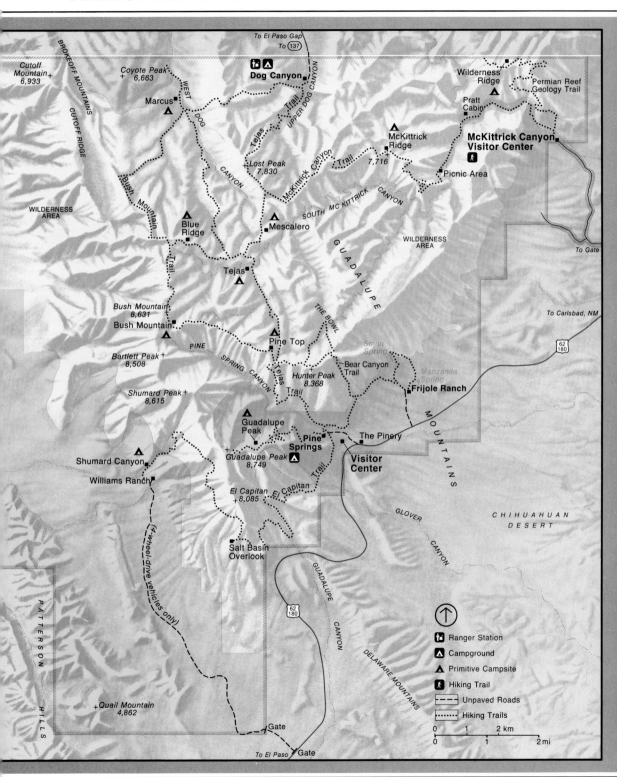

To El Paso Gap
To (137)

Cutoff
Mountain +
6,933

BRONKEOFF MOUNTAINS

CUTOFF RIDGE

Coyote Peak +
6,663

Marcus

WEST DOG CANYON

Dog Canyon

UPPER DOG CANYON

Tejas Trail

Wilderness
Ridge

Permian Reef
Geology Trail

Pratt
Cabin

McKittrick
Ridge
+ 7,716

McKittrick Canyon
Visitor Center

Picnic Area

Lost Peak
7,830

McKittrick Canyon Trail

WILDERNESS
AREA

Bush Mountain Trail

Blue
Ridge

Mescalero

SOUTH MC KITTRICK CANYON

G U A D A L U P E

WILDERNESS
AREA

To Gate

Tejas

Bush Mountain
8,631 +

Bush Mountain

PINE

Pine Top

THE BOWL

Smith
Spring

Bear Canyon
Trail

Manzanita
Spring

Frijole Ranch

To Carlsbad, NM

62
180

SPRING CANYON

Tejas Trail

Hunter Peak
8,368

Bartlett Peak +
8,508

Shumard Peak +
8,615

Guadalupe
Peak

Pine
Springs

The Pinery

M O U N T A I N S

Shumard Canyon

+
Guadalupe Peak
8,749

Visitor
Center

Williams Ranch

El Capitan Trail

El Capitan
+ 8,085

GLOVER CANYON

CHIHUAHUAN
DESERT

(4-wheel-drive vehicles only)

Salt Basin
Overlook

GUADALUPE CANYON

P
A
T
T
E
R
S
O
N

H
I
L
L
S

62
180

DELAWARE MOUNTAINS

+ Quail Mountain
4,862

Gate

To El Paso Gate

[↑]

🚹 Ranger Station
▲ Campground
🔺 Primitive Campsite
🚶 Hiking Trail
- - - Unpaved Roads
····· Hiking Trails

0   1   2 km
0   1   2 mi

has spread as far east as it's likely to go; and the eastern chinquapin oak is living on the fringe of its western range.

Screened by trees, the creek flowed unseen. I heard it before the trail reached it. A shallow stream slipped from one clear pool to the next at the crossing. Lime deposits coated the creek bed, reflecting a pale blue sky. The trail meandered through the ribbon of trees that hugged the water, passing bigtooth maple and velvet ash. In this season all were shades of green. Occasionally a shadow flittered through the higher branches as a bird changed its perch. But most of the canyon's abundant wildlife waited in the shade or underground for the sun to pass overhead.

As the canyon walls narrowed, each turn revealed a shift in topography. On one side, steep talus slopes buried much of the bedrock. On the other, massive cliffs, rough-cut and fluted, overlooked the canyon floor. A black fringe of desert varnish streaked the tops of the gray walls.

A FEW MILES from the trailhead, I reached the Pratt Cabin at the junction of the north and south branches of McKittrick Canyon. The place was a geologist's dream. Everything was built of stone—thick blocks for the walls, thinner slices for the roof. In front of the house sat an immense slab set on stubby stone legs for a table. Stopping to take a break, I let the pack slip from my shoulders with a thud.

The cabin had been home to Wallace E. Pratt, who first wandered up the creek in the early 1920s. The young geologist put aside his search for oil long enough to visit the remote canyon rumored to be the most beautiful place in Texas. He not only agreed when he saw McKittrick, but went one step further. "It was," he said, "the most beautiful spot I'd ever seen."

As I sat at Pratt's table, I thought about the man whose life became so intertwined with these mountains. Pratt was the first geologist hired by Humble Oil, which later became part of Exxon. He knew where to find oil and eventually became vice president of the company. Yet he spent many summers in this isolated cabin, fascinated by the natural beauty around him. He became an ardent conservationist and prime mover behind the creation of a wilderness preserve in the Guadalupe Mountains. The petroleum geologist donated more than 5,000 acres in McKittrick Canyon to form the nucleus of the national park.

Pratt saw more than pretty scenery when he sat here gazing at the massive cliffs. McKittrick Creek had exposed one of the most extensive fossil reefs in the world. The limestone deposits in the Capitan Reef recorded life in a Permian sea 250 million years ago. They also may have given Pratt a few ideas about where to search for oil.

Enormous colonies of lime-secreting algae and sponges formed the reef, several hundred miles long, on the fringe of a shallow inland sea. When the arm of the sea where the reef grew was cut off from the larger ocean, it evaporated, and minerals distilled from seawater buried the reef. Over millions of years, the tremendous pressure of overlying rock transformed the remains of marine organisms into oil. As the land rose, the softer rock eroded away, and the petroleum pockets drained. But uplift exposed only some portions of the ancient reef; those that stayed buried retained deposits of oil. Geologists still come to the Guadalupes in droves, crawling over the cliffs, studying the structure of the rock outcrops. The exposed reef provides clues to oil-bearing beds hidden beneath the surface farther east.

Taking up the trail again, I passed a shallow depression ringed with stone. It was an old mescal pit used by Indians for roasting the hearts of the spiky-leafed agave, also known as mescal. Mescalero Apache, who arrived in the Guadalupes about 600 years ago, take their name from the plant, once one of their primary foods. The agave matures for 8 to 20 years, then suddenly sends up a tall stalk in a single burst of growth before it flowers and dies. Apache families gathered the plants in late spring and roasted them during a four-day ceremony.

Before the hike, I had spent a day gathering mescal with Evelyn Martine, a Mescalero Apache in her 80s. We had gone with Mark Rosacker from the Living Desert State Park in Carlsbad to a ranch in the foothills of the Guadalupes. "Mescal gives you power," Martine said. "It makes you strong. That plant is good. That's why, old as I am, I walk all around."

Before the first plant was gathered, Martine gave a long prayer in Apache requesting the mescal to continue growing so others could return to use it. She watched as I pried loose a stout agave and began hacking at the basal leaves. "This is how you do it," she said, taking the hatchet. She quickly chopped off the leaves with strong, clean strokes, letting me carry the enormous yellow heart to the truck. As we walked back, Martine mentioned that she had been born in a tepee. "Thinking back," she said, "there are lots of changes. We lived in a tepee with one fire for cooking and heat. Then tents with a cast-iron stove. Now houses. I went from horses to wagons and now to cars and pickups."

I continued hiking up the south fork of McKittrick to a long talus slope leading out of the canyon. Climbing the switchbacks, I stopped several times to lighten my load of water. Below, the green corridor along the creek linked the dry mountains with the drier desert. Tall ponderosa pines grew in a sheltered pocket near a deep pool. From the pool trickled a dark vein of water that soon disappeared beneath the gravels.

A rooftop among the trees marked the site of the Hunter lodge. Judge J. C. Hunter had put together a large ranch in the

Guadalupes by acquiring smaller ranches during the Depression; these included Frijole, the oldest homestead in the park, built by cattlemen in the 1870s. Like his neighbor, Wallace Pratt, Judge Hunter vigorously promoted the idea of a national park.

"We kept care of the place real good—I thought we did," said Noel Kincaid, the ranch foreman for J. C. Hunter. Kincaid now makes his home in Carlsbad. He had been born more than 70 years before on the north side of the Guadalupes in a dugout—a makeshift dwelling scooped from the side of a hill. Soft-spoken, dressed in faded jeans and a snap-button western shirt, he gave an impression of solid competence. Mounted heads of deer, elk, and bighorn sheep stared down from the walls of his living room, along with a portrait of John Wayne.

At first, Kincaid had been worried when the National Park Service bought Hunter's 70,000-acre Guadalupe Mountains Ranch. He envisioned paved roads and parking lots destroying the beauty of the remote range he knew so well. "The people who want to visit the Guadalupes," he said, looking at me with a steady gaze, "the people who want to see nature as God made it, can hike in or ride in." Kincaid had ridden the Guadalupes in all varieties of weather—sometimes on the same day. Once he took a good rock horse up the Bear Canyon Trail from the Frijole Ranch. Frijole was headquarters for Hunter's huge estate, and Kincaid, as ranch foreman, lived there with his family. "Left in the rain," he recounted. "Snow on top. By the time I got to the west crest, the wind's ablowin' and the sand's aflyin'. I sat out there where they used to have the weather station and watched that needle rock back and forth from 100 to 120 miles per hour."

NOEL'S SON JACK, who was born and raised at Frijole, works for the Park Service as a packer. Several times a week he leads a string of mules and horses into the mountains, carrying supplies needed by backcountry patrols. I talked with him one morning in the corrals at the Frijole Ranch, now part of the park. Wearing spurs, a handlebar mustache, and his ranger uniform, Jack was balancing loads on the back of a nervous mule.

"Sometimes they call me head packer," he said as he placed a water container on the pack saddle. " 'Course I'm the *only* packer," he added with a smile. The younger Kincaid spoke gently to his mule as he continued loading. He was on a first-name basis with all the animals, having spent long days with them on his solitary trips into the mountains. "Yes," he admitted, "I talk to the mules. I even talk to me sometimes—that's all I get to listen to."

Loud voices drifted up from McKittrick Creek as a brightly clad group of students on a field trip made its way up the trail. They were the first hikers I had seen. Two boys pulled away from the rest and jogged past wearing only shorts and baseball hats, traveling light. I glanced at my boulder-size pack and wondered if I wasn't doing it all wrong. But a half hour later I passed them huddled in the thin shade of a juniper, worn out. After giving the runners some water, I continued up the trail, bent under the pack, head tucked down.

When I looked up to check the route, I saw a burst of red on a far cliff—a detonation of color in a landscape bleached by the high-noon sun. It was a claret cup cactus in full, primal bloom growing from the vertical rock. After a few more switchbacks I reached the ridgetop, where I dumped the pack. Billowing clouds, as flat-bottomed as the horizon and as rough-topped as the walls of the canyon, gathered far out over the desert.

I had planned to camp here, but once in the uplands—with the scent of pine needles in the air, with the sun still high, without a wall or a roof between me and hundreds of miles of open country—I couldn't stop. Picking up the pack, which felt heavier than before, I continued walking. The trail undulated across McKittrick Ridge through the wide light of the high country.

Taking a detour to the top of Lost Peak, I gazed north across ridges rolling down the back of the Guadalupes into the desert below. A lower rise hid the Dog Canyon ranger station. Earlier, I had driven the hundred miles from park headquarters to the Dog Canyon outpost. I wanted to meet Roger Reisch, who had rangered in the Guadalupes for more than a quarter of a century. He had lived for ten years at Frijole Ranch after the Kincaids left and the ranch became parkland. Like Noel Kincaid, he believes in keeping the park undeveloped. "Once you have the access," he said, "the remoteness is gone."

Reisch relaxed in his home among a collection of cowboy hats—at least one for each season. He mentioned that hikers use the backcountry at all times of the year. In winter, deep snows fall in the higher elevations of the park. Winter backpackers used to carry minimal gear, he said. They dressed in Levi's, carried a tarp instead of a tent, and wore bread wrappers on their heads to shed the wet snow. "Now," he said, "they come in with good winter gear." His face lit up when he began talking about the mountains that had become his home. "Beautiful sights," he said. "I can take them every day."

Returning from Lost Peak, I continued along the trail until I reached Mescalero Camp—one of the park's designated backcountry camps—just before dark. The evening air stood dead still as browsing deer rustled in the dry oak leaves on the slope below camp. Trees grow thick here at the head of South McKittrick Canyon. The folds of the higher ridges shelter limber pine and Douglas fir, rare this far south. The heaviest stands of these trees grow within a shaded basin known as The Bowl. They are remnants of a coniferous forest that covered west Texas during the Ice Age. As *(Continued on page 134)*

*H*unter Peak stands watch above the northern fringes of the
Chihuahuan Desert, where jointed walkingstick cholla and spiky
soaptree yucca spread across the arid grasslands. Here the warning
rattle of a northern blacktail rattlesnake (opposite) keeps predators at a
distance, and the agave's bristling points, coated with a mild toxin, deter
browsers. But life in the desert must attract as well as repel. The brilliant
red flowers of the claret cup cactus lure insects necessary for pollination.

CARR CLIFTON

MATT BRADLEY

Williams Ranch (left), dwarfed by its mountainous backdrop, stands empty at the foot of the western escarpment of the Guadalupes. Overgrazed by Longhorn cattle and sheep, the land has begun to recover as native grasses slowly return. Only crumbling walls remain of The Pinery (above), built in 1858 as a fortified stage station on the Butterfield Overland Mail Line. Passengers stopped here to stretch their legs and dine on venison pie.

*P*ale limbs of a Texas madrone curve skyward in McKittrick Canyon. As the tree grows, its red bark stretches and splits into papery shreds that peel away, exposing a smooth, white underbark. Madrones may be on the decline in the Guadalupes. Some produce abundant berries in the fall, but few of the seeds germinate, and fewer seedlings survive. Crimson berries (right) cluster on a madrone in Dog Canyon, where a black-chinned hummingbird hovers, one of 260 bird species in the park.

RALPH LEE HOPKINS

conditions grew more arid and the desert spread northward, the re-treating forest left behind a relict stand in the high mountains. Elk, once hunted to extinction but reintroduced during the 1920s by Judge Hunter, wander through the forest.

The great wedge of mountains cutting deep into the dry country was long a sanctuary for the Apache. When military pressure against the Indians increased after the Civil War, the Guadalupes became the last refuge of the Mescalero. Soldiers regularly scoured the range, burning villages and keeping the Apache bands on the run.

In January 1870, 200 black cavalrymen known as Buffalo Soldiers attacked a Mescalero encampment in a remote region northeast of Pine Springs. The Apache retreated to a high peak, where they made a stand. The troopers dismounted and began ascending under heavy fire from above. Just before dark they reached the summit as the Indians withdrew, leaving behind ten of their dead.

A large cavalry force returned in the spring to sweep the mountains clear of the Apache. The broken terrain and a maze of confusing trails baffled the guides, who soon became lost. But the soldiers pressed on, finding abandoned villages in almost every canyon. They surprised an occupied camp of 75 lodges in a hidden ravine and destroyed large quantities of supplies. But the operation took its toll on the soldiers. Half the horsemen stumbled back to the fort on foot, having lost their mounts in the rugged territory.

Just before full dark I heard the ponderous whop-whop-whop of large wings overhead. A black shape swooped through the trees and landed heavily on the top limb of a snag, sitting humped against the dark sky. A moment later its partner appeared, circling above. The tips of its outstretched wings rocked back and forth in an aerial balancing act—the signature of a turkey vulture. The first bird jumped off its perch, and both disappeared into the shadows below.

*T*HE NEXT MORNING, as the sun broke over the eastern rim, I headed up the mountain toward Blue Ridge. An elk had left tracks in the powdery dust of the trail the night before; two mule deer startled at my approach and loped away. Topping a high shoulder, I heard a wild turkey letting loose with a deep-throated *gobbledy gobble-gobble*. The bird was somewhere close, calling to a second turkey, which answered from the next ridge. I rounded a bend of the trail and stopped. A red-wattled gobbler strutted toward me with its mottled tail feathers fanned out, lost in its own thoughts. Suddenly it noticed what shared its path and scrambled into the woods with a last wild gobble.

Ridges climbed to the south and west, the geology hidden beneath thick soil and heavy timber. I continued westward under an expanding sky until all at once the world fell away. The ridge I was following disappeared, sheared off in a great precipice. It was as if someone had taken a knife and sliced the mountain in half. The contrast was remarkable. One moment the land was heavily forested, rising steadily in rounded contours. The next, it dropped thousands of feet, changing abruptly from rolling uplands into stark desert.

Nearly a mile lower than the summit of the Guadalupes the barren Salt Basin spread along the western base of the escarpment. To the south, brush-anchored red sands pushed toward a line of white gypsum dunes, sweeping upward in 60-foot crests. Locals say the two sands never mix, no matter how hard the wind blows. The dunes lie on a ranch belonging to the Lynch brothers. In the tradition of Pratt and Hunter, they want to see the place protected.

"We realized it was a rare area that needed preserving," Jim Lynch told me when I talked with him in his Dell City office. "There's lots of open country," he added, "but this is unique." Only a few places in the world have the right combination of gypsum deposits, strong winds, and dry climate needed to form gypsum sand dunes. Congress authorized an expansion of the park to include the dune fields, but transfer of the land has not been completed. Jim Lynch wants to see the dunes come under Park Service protection. "The area itself is so beautiful, so fragile," he said, "that we preserved it ourselves all these years."

I headed along the trail and reached the summit of Bush Mountain. Originally I had planned to camp here on the second night, but it was only late morning. Guadalupe Peak reared up several rough, broken miles farther south. The topography was steep and the footing loose, but the great palisade I had been following pointed that way. I decided to continue along the crest. Hours later, the terrain was beginning to take its toll as I approached the south side of Guadalupe Peak. Stopping to rest without bothering to remove the pack, I slumped into a catatonic state, but soon forced myself to start moving, just to let the vultures know I was alive. The route I followed brought me to a break in the knife-edge ridge below the peak. The sheer west faces of Guadalupe and El Capitan fell away into the same empty space. Wind rushed through the gap as I looked over the edge, holding my hat.

Far below lay the Williams Ranch, a solitary structure overwhelmed by the sheer mass of raw cliffs. Years of grinding wind had left little more than an artifact of a homesteader's desperate dream. In 1908 Robert Belcher built the wood-frame ranch house for his bride. After riding two days beyond the nearest neighbor, she took one look at her new home and her heart sank. The next morning she left for the East, never to return.

Dolph Williams bought the property in 1915 and raised goats with an Indian named—like many hereabouts—Geronimo. Williams was still working his holdings in the 1930s when Loren Eiseley, then a young anthropologist, spent the summer excavating a cave on his ranch. Eiseley was part of a team searching for evidence of Paleo-Indians dating back to the end of the Ice Age. They thought their chances of success were good, since caves in the Guadalupes had yielded the remains of Pleistocene animals. One site near the rim of the western escarpment contained bones of musk-oxen, perhaps dragged there by saber-toothed cats whose remains lay nearby.

Eiseley dug a trench across the cave floor and near the far wall uncovered the burial of an infant wrapped on a cradle board, carefully swaddled in soft buckskin painted red. He felt that taking the child from its resting place would be a desecration. But, fearing its eventual destruction by pothunters, he removed the burial. Years later, the literary anthropologist had second thoughts. "Something told me," he wrote, "that the child and its accouterments should have been left where the parents intended before they departed, left to the endless circling of the stars beyond the cavern mouth and the entering shaft of sun by day. This for all eternity."

*F*ARTHER SOUTH from the Williams Ranch, the highway crosses the Salt Basin at Salt Flat some 15 miles from the park. I had spent a couple of hours there before my hike, talking with Ben and Isobel Gilmore. An immense pair of mounted long horns hung on the wall of the living room. Ben had ranched most of his life and had served as a justice of the peace; Isobel and Ben had run the café in Salt Flat after a drought forced them to sell their cattle herd. Born and raised there, Isobel talked about the wind.

"We've been having these old winds," she said. Gusts had reached more than 110 miles an hour the month before. "It's been terrible. One wind came up and rattled the window, shakin' it back and forth. Blew the putty clean off." She ran to hold the pane in the frame, calling Ben to help. Just then she heard a tremendous noise. "Oh Lord," she said, "please don't let that be my roof." The pane fell to the ground and broke as she hurried out to check the roof. It had weathered the storm, but four trees had toppled and the wind had stripped the ground clean. "The dirt had done gone—just left the gravel."

The wind continued to funnel through the notch where I stood. I soon moved on, following a faint deer trail up the side of Guadalupe Peak. The route ended at the base of a sheer cliff. I thought I'd have to backtrack to the wind gap and find another way, but then I spotted a few deer tracks passing around the corner of the rock face. They soon led to the main trail coming up from the visitor center at Pine Springs. Although close to the summit, I wanted to save the top for sunrise, so I turned toward the park's camping area a mile below.

On the way down, the pathway skirted a mescal pit on a narrow saddle. Two thousand feet directly below, a green patch marked the location of a spring. After gathering mescal, Evelyn Martine and her companion, Mary Peña, had led me there—a place sacred to the Mescalero. Martine had filled water containers to take home with her for healing. An Apache story tells of singing and drumming that once came from a cave perched high on a cliff near the spring. Against all advice, a medicine woman climbed to the entrance and disappeared. Her people gave her up for dead. But a long time later she returned, bringing with her the power to cure.

That night in camp, I lay awake, listening to the wind shake the tent and spill over the shoulder of the mountain. "Guadalupe Peak is one of our medicine mountains," Elbys Hugar had told me when I visited her on the Mescalero Apache Reservation outside the park. A great-granddaughter of the 19th-century Apache chief Cochise, Hugar runs the tribal museum. "Every now and then these people go out to Guadalupe Peak. They go there to pray. They feel better. There is a place where people can hear singing down below, beneath the rocks. Have you heard it?" she asked. I told her no, I had not. "It's nothing to be afraid of if you hear it." She explained that the singing comes from friendly mountain spirits that are impersonated by masked dancers in towering headdresses during a girl's coming-of-age ceremony. "We believe in them to heal the sick, to drive away evil spirits, to bless the people and bless the home. It is one of the traditions we still carry today. It's part of us, part of our lives."

Wind continued to sweep the mountain early the next morning. I drank the last of my water and picked my way up the trail in the dark. Near the summit, I ducked out of the wind, waiting until closer to sunrise before going the rest of the way. Sitting there in the growing light, I began thinking about Noel Kincaid, who was born in a dugout, and about Evelyn Martine, born in a tepee. I thought about the Apache, the ranchers, the park rangers—all those whose lives had become part of the Guadalupes. This had always been their mountain. Watching the broken line of the cliffs emerge from the darkness, I decided not to go on. I would leave the summit to them.

Stars fell beneath the western escarpment as a lens of light spread across the distant horizon. Soon the sun broke over the dark immensity of the desert. And it wasn't long after that I began thinking about a cup of coffee. Retracing my steps down the mountain, I packed my gear and headed for the Nickel Creek Café.

FOLLOWING PAGES: Wind-ribbed gypsum dunes swell beneath the broken skyline of the Guadalupes' western escarpment. Transfer of these rare dune fields to Guadalupe Mountains National Park is under way.

DAVID MUENCH

High above McKittrick Canyon, a hiker pauses to take a photograph at the top of the Permian Reef Geology Trail. Switchbacking 2,000 feet above the canyon floor, the trail gives amateur and professional geologists a close look at rocks that form one of the most

*extensive fossil reefs in the world. McKittrick Creek (opposite), the only
perennial stream in the park, has cut a deep cross section through the
ancient reef. Here a lone ponderosa pine, usually found at higher
elevations, grows at streamside near stands of bigtooth maple.*

"Frost has set in," wrote Col. Benjamin H. Grierson when he explored McKittrick Canyon in 1878, *"and the great variety of tints and hues of foliage, from dark green to pure carmine, added greatly to the life and beauty of the magnificent scenery."* Nomadic Indians began visiting the region 11,000 years before the army officer but left little evidence of their passing. Calcium carbonate deposits partially obscure a pictograph of unknown age on a canyon wall.

TOM ALGIRE

El Capitan catches the warm light of late afternoon above a vast sweep of west Texas. East of the 8,085-foot-high bluff, geophysicists (above) examine a portion of the ancient reef that forms the backbone of the Guadalupe Mountains. The fossil of a marine organism, one of nearly 500 fossil species found within the park, yields clues to life in the shallow sea that covered this region 250 million years ago.

RALPH LEE HOPKINS (RIGHT)

Biscayne
Subtropical Island Realm

By Jennifer C. Urquhart

Photographs by Stephen Frink and Medford Taylor

BRIGHT SUNLIGHT pierces crystalline water, refracting into countless diamonds on the white sand below. I glide slowly through a school of silversides, thousands of them, hundreds of thousands, tiny, iridescent, moving as one body. The tide is out; the scintillating creatures have abandoned their now-exposed hiding places among the mangrove roots lining the nearby shore, perhaps to seek camouflage in the dappled noontime light. A largish barracuda and several smaller ones, languid and disinterested, circle the fishy mass.

Ahead of my fingertips tiny fish slip in waves. I am a maestro conducting a symphony; instead of musical notes, these glistening creatures move at my will—sometimes turning in darting presto tempo, sometimes in stately adagio. I half expect to be tickled by them as we swim along together. But no. Like disembodied beings they slide past, without any contact.

I swim over turtle-grass beds and algae called mermaid's wine glass, looking like tiny doll's cups. Bright orange, toxic fire sponges lie a little deeper. A brittle star waves delicate arms from its sheltering vase sponge. Now I peer down at the half-buried skeletal remains of an old vessel, transformed into weird sculpture by a cloak of algae, sponges, and other living things. In the shelter of its keel and ribs parades a colorful array of fish: a small parrotfish, pinkish juvenile mangrove snappers with jaunty eye stripes, a brilliant yellow-and-black damselfish. On part of the wreck that emerges from the water a cormorant perches, hanging its wings out to dry. It takes off at my approach, clumsily scudding its feet in the water before becoming airborne. Later I daydream on the beach, watching boaters, white-clad—like an image out of F. Scott Fitzgerald's *The Great Gatsby*—row a sleek wooden skiff from their sailboat anchored offshore.

Sporting white-phase plumage typical of the species in Florida, a great blue heron stalks prey at the edge of the mangroves.

PRECEDING PAGES: Underwater fantasy world captivates a snorkeler at Biscayne National Park in south Florida. The park protects such living coral reefs, which here reach their northern limit in the United States.

MEDFORD TAYLOR (OPPOSITE); STEPHEN FRINK (PRECEDING PAGES)

I had been snorkeling off the beach at Elliott Key in Biscayne National Park in south Florida. Elliott, largest of the 45 islands in the 181,500-acre park, rises at its highest to about eight feet above sea level. Ninety-five percent of the park's acreage lies underwater.

On a clear day on Biscayne Bay, you get a sensation of passing through Alice's looking glass: Where does water end and land begin? Are you really paddling around in a pristine, blue-green subtropical paradise, or is this part of bustling Miami, whose skyline drifts on the horizon 15 miles to the north? Biscayne is indeed an urban park. Mount Trashmore, a major landfill 150 feet high—the highest point of land in Dade County—nudges the edge of the park, as do the stacks of the Turkey Point nuclear plant. On Columbus Day weekend, partying crowds gather, perhaps 40,000 strong. The beginning of lobster season in midsummer brings almost as many. "You can walk from boat to boat then, across the bay," one woman told me.

But there is a wildness here, too. Many times you go for hours without seeing another boat. Rare turtles nest in the park. Manatees linger in these waters in winter. The endangered American crocodile finds refuge in the vicinity. The Chaus swallowtail butterfly, also endangered, breeds on several of the islands. And here that most vivid treasure, the living coral reef, reaches its farthest northern extension in the United States. "It's a natural area about as pretty as anything you'll ever see," says L. Wayne Landrum, former chief ranger, "with the longest stretch of undeveloped shore on Florida's east coast."

*H*OW CAN A PARK so close to a metropolis of almost two million people remain wild and, seemingly, little known? Part of the reason is simply nomenclature; generations of Miamians know well this vast, watery expanse in the shadow of the much better known Everglades National Park. They just consider Biscayne Bay their own local recreation area. They don't know that much of it has now been designated a national park. Such might not have been the case, however. Except for the work of many dedicated people in the early 1960s, these waters, coral reefs, and last few undeveloped keys in southern Florida might have come to resemble a Gulf Coast industrial strip or a Miami Beach condo alley, instead of the clear blue waters and white coralline shores I found.

One name that kept coming up in my travels was that of Dante B. Fascell, retired U. S. congressman from south Florida.

"Little known!" scoffs the 37-year veteran of Capitol Hill, balking at that description of Biscayne National Park—which is clearly one of his favorite subjects. "It ought to be *better* known." In the early sixties Biscayne was certainly on the congressman's mind, and before that, too. "All my life, until I actually got into the legislature and the

BISCAYNE NATIONAL PARK

LOCATION: Florida
ESTABLISHED: June 28, 1980
SIZE: 181,500 acres

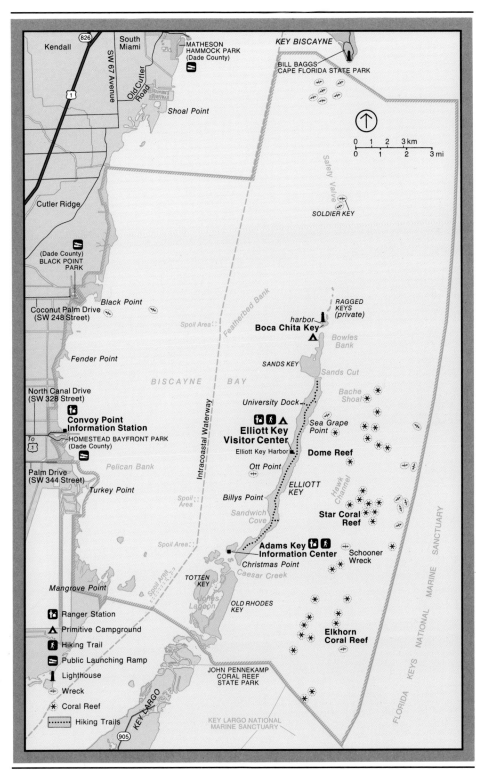

826
Kendall
South Miami
SW 67 Avenue
SW 67 Avenue
Old Cutler Road
MATHESON HAMMOCK PARK (Dade County)
KEY BISCAYNE
BILL BAGGS CAPE FLORIDA STATE PARK
Shoal Point
1
Cutler Ridge
Safety Valve
SOLDIER KEY
0 1 2 3 km
0 1 2 3 mi
(Dade County) BLACK POINT PARK
Black Point
Coconut Palm Drive (SW 248 Street)
Featherbed Bank
RAGGED KEYS (private)
harbor
Boca Chita Key
Bowles Bank
Spoil Area
Fender Point
SANDS KEY
Sands Cut
BISCAYNE BAY
North Canal Drive (SW 328 Street)
Convoy Point Information Station
Intracoastal Waterway
University Dock
Bache Shoal
Sea Grape Point
Elliott Key Visitor Center
Dome Reef
To US 1
HOMESTEAD BAYFRONT PARK (Dade County)
Elliott Key Harbor
Pelican Bank
Ott Point
Palm Drive (SW 344 Street)
ELLIOTT KEY
Hawk Channel
Turkey Point
Spoil Area
Billys Point
Star Coral Reef
Sandwich Cove
Spoil Area
Adams Key Information Center
Schooner Wreck
Christmas Point
Caesar Creek
Mangrove Point
Spoil Area
TOTTEN KEY
Jones Lagoon
OLD RHODES KEY
Ranger Station
Primitive Campground
Hiking Trail
Public Launching Ramp
Lighthouse
Wreck
Coral Reef
Hiking Trails
Elkhorn Coral Reef
JOHN PENNEKAMP CORAL REEF STATE PARK
KEY LARGO
905
KEY LARGO NATIONAL MARINE SANCTUARY
BISCAYNE NATIONAL MARINE SANCTUARY
FLORIDA KEYS

Congress, Biscayne Bay was just like my front yard. I spent a lot of time on those islands," says Fascell, who has remained a strong advocate of conservation. "As a youngster, I was always out on the bay. It sort of ties in with your youth. I'd hate to have it despoiled."

Many people give the congressman a large share of credit for the park's existence. "It was a tough struggle," recalls Fascell. "I had to fight at least two campaigns that I know of on the issue." The winning of this battle marked a big change, he thinks, tipping the balance in Florida toward protection of the environment rather than overdevelopment. Fascell credits the community for getting behind that effort. A huge petrochemical complex was defeated. It was harder to stop Islandia, the city dreamed up by developers for these unpopulated islands. The plan was to build a ten-mile-long causeway from Key Biscayne to the chain of islands, then to fill them, and portions of the bay, with hotels and resorts. The debate raged on: park or development—or both?

"Until we finally said, to hell. There is no way you can do this halfway," the congressman remembers. "You've just got to make it all a park. You've got to preserve the bay. You've got to include the reefs. You've got to include all the islands."

And so in 1968 much of Biscayne Bay was set aside as Biscayne National Monument, and in 1980 the bill turning it into a national park was signed. In 1990 the Florida Keys National Marine Sanctuary was set up, encompassing all of the keys. Its charter declares some of the region, especially around reefs, an "Area to be Avoided" by large vessels and forbids oil and gas development in waters adjacent to the park.

AT THE DOCK near park headquarters on Convoy Point, I boarded *Reef Rover IV,* one of the two large glass-bottom boats that take visitors out over the reefs. The phenomenon of a coral reef depends on a rare combination of warm, clear, and relatively wave-free waters. They must be nutrient-*poor* waters—to prevent the proliferation of algae, which would stop enough sunlight from reaching the corals. Hard and soft coral formations vary greatly in color and shape. Soft corals form flexible, branching colonies, while hard corals are the foundation stones of the reef. Each hard coral is a conglomeration of countless tiny, soft-bodied animals called polyps, which attach themselves to a firm surface. They feed, mostly at night, by grasping even more minute plants and creatures with their tentacles and dropping them into their mouths. The polyps secrete calcium carbonate—the building material of reefs—surrounding themselves with cuplike skeletons that fuse together. When they die, their limestone skeletons remain part of the reef. Corals also live in other waters, but only in these optimum conditions are they able, as naturalist Rachel Carson said, "to turn the substance of the sea into rock."

Capt. Ed Davidson runs the glass-bottom boats. An ex-Navy jet fighter pilot and staunch environmentalist, he has worked hard to preserve the Florida Keys and their reefs. He educates visitors about the reefs and the problems of overdevelopment in the region, as evidenced by such phenomena as "Florida's most wildly growing species, *Condominius giganticus.*" He also explains that the northern Florida Keys are actually a line of 100,000-year-old coral reefs. The sea level in those days was 25 feet higher than now. What are now keys were then submerged coral reefs. "At that time," says Captain Ed, "the southern tip of Florida was in Orlando—Mickey Mouse was underwater!"

In this subtropical world *ice,* strangely enough, had a role. During the last ice age, continental glaciers advancing south locked up a lot of seawater in ice, and the sea level dropped 150 feet. The exposed coral reefs died off, and their calcareous skeletons formed the islands we see today.

No amount of dry geology can prepare you for a living reef. Some call it the undersea equivalent of a tropical rain forest, because of its complexity and diversity of species. On a windy day we anchored off a sheltered patch reef. Soon I floated mask down, mesmerized by the delicate array. Soft corals took form as fans and plumes and whips, in shades of purples and oranges, pinks and yellows, swaying with utmost grace in the slight surge. The more calcareous hard corals, staghorn and elkhorn, rose in jagged, branching tiers toward the surface, above great boulders of brain corals and star corals. *Cabezas de los Mártires,* Spanish explorers called these reefs—Heads of the Martyrs— whose sharp teeth tore into the sides of unwary ships.

Diving closer, I discerned other creatures in a busy, technicolor world: sponges, sea cucumbers, brittle stars, tube worms, feather duster worms, gorgonians arranged in miniature gardens atop brain coral boulders. Fish in jewel colors and fanciful shapes fed unconcernedly or shyly retreated at my passing shadow into crevices and sheltering overhangs. A queen angelfish, with a circular turquoise "crown" above the eyes, boldly inspected me. A gray angelfish passed by with its graceful trailing fin. Yellow snappers swam in loose formation. Bold-striped sergeant majors performed snappy martial routines.

Corals, I learned, are not the only island builders here. The park's mangrove trees fringe islands and mainland in a dense, uninviting tangle of slimy roots and branches. It is almost impenetrable. I know, because I tried it, climbing along roots and limbs. The role of mangroves is as important, however, as that of corals. Columbus saw mangroves, describing in 1494 "trees that grow down to the sea, which shows that no storm ever reaches there. . . ." Columbus clearly had never experienced a hurricane in this area. He noted the roots were "covered with oysters innumerable." Sir Walter Raleigh later claimed the mangroves actually grew oysters. *(Continued on page 160)*

Islands in the sun sprawl across Biscayne Bay. Though such mangrove-covered keys and a mainland fringe encompass only about 5 percent of this watery park, they form an important ecological component. Tangles of mangroves shelter abundant life, and shield keys, bay, and mainland from waves and storms. In a camping program on Adams Key (island with dock), a local schoolgirl looks through a glass-bottom bucket for sea creatures. Park staff aim to instill wonder at the area's rare ecosystem.

MEDFORD TAYLOR (BOTH)

*S*pindly root "legs" carry pioneering red mangroves across the water to build up new land by trapping debris. Other plants will eventually colonize this acreage. Mangroves clarify the water and offer a haven for myriad oysters, sponges, anemones, and juvenile fish—as well as good hunting for the tricolor heron. Its outstretched wings may shade water to improve visibility of prey. A mangrove canopy (above), beneath which a boatman poles his skiff, provides nesting habitat for birds.

JEFF FOOTT; MEDFORD TAYLOR (ABOVE); STEPHEN FRINK (OPPOSITE)

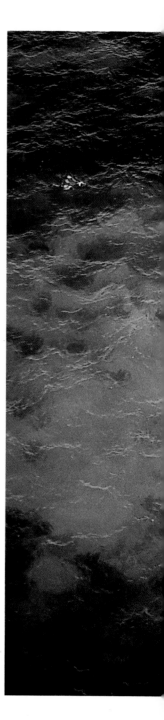

BRIAN PARKER / TOM STACK & ASSOCIATES; MEDFORD TAYLOR (ABOVE AND RIGHT)

*S*norkelers *of all ages test reef waters a few miles offshore.*
Reef Rover IV *(above, right) tugs at an anchor carefully placed to avoid*
cutting into slow-growing coral reefs and turtle-grass beds. Through
glass panels on the 53-foot, shallow-draft vessel, concessionaire Capt. Ed

*Davidson (opposite, top) points out sea life on the bay floor. Two such
boats operate in the park, carrying snorkelers, scuba divers, and other
passengers to islands and offshore reefs. Using two large boats instead of
many small ones reduces the number and impact of anchorings.*

Gary Bremen, park ranger, explained that mangroves protect the coast and that there are some curious adaptations in the three different species—red, black, and white—commonly found here. "All are salt water tolerant," he said, "but each type handles it differently. The red mangrove's roots and leaves don't take in salt at all. The leaf's waxy coat protects it." I fingered heavy, magnolia-like leaves. "The black mangrove exudes the salt water through the leaf surface. It looks wet most of the time, but on a windy day it looks whitish from the dried salt. The white mangrove, which grows farther up out of the water, has two little glands at the base of the leaf. The plant exudes salt through them.

"The red mangrove tree is the most obvious in appearance," said Gary. "It's the one that you see right at water's edge." It has an ingenious way of spreading, which, along with regeneration from its seeds, results in island building. Sometimes dubbed "walking trees," the pioneering red mangroves take giant steps across the water on long, stiltlike prop roots. Leaves and debris gradually collect and build up under the arching roots until at long last terra firma is created and, in the words of one writer, "the squish becomes solid earth."

The mangrove is also important as a water filter, trapping silt and impurities as they pass through the mass of roots and detritus. The trees add a lot of nutrients, too. The mangroves' role as habitat for numerous critters, such as Columbus's oysters and immature fish, became evident one afternoon off Sands Key. In gin-clear water cleansed by the mangroves, we nosed with our snorkels into the tangle of prop roots, which creaked with the rising tide. Each bower of roots was like a little neighborhood. A school of tiny fish sheltered in one barrio. In the next swam grunts, yellow-striped over blue. Across the way grazed a large group of parrotfish, vivid turquoise and green, with cobalt blue beaklike teeth that they use to bite off chunks of coral and eat algae and coral polyps.

*H*EADING ACROSS the nearby turtle grass that stretched like a miniature expanse of saw grass, I found elfin gardens, with neptune's shaving brush algae for little trees, sponges for hillocks, and waving fingers of purple anemones set artfully here and there. In this grassy expanse crawled a sea hare, a kind of sea slug. Pale olive with dark rings, it resembled a chunky worm in a ruffly, polka-dotted pinafore. To befuddle predators, I am told, it squirts out purple juice. This one continued its tranquil progress at a pace more tortoise- than hare-like.

On another day, I joined a group of elementary school children on Adams Key in one of the environmental education programs the Park Service runs for local schools. "Get 'em when they're young," said park ranger Christine Rogers, who was supervising the program. "My theme is that not only the ranger can take care of the park. It's theirs, too. I ask them to become park rangers!"

With nature walks, scavenger hunts, and other games lively enough to keep a bunch of active kids absorbed, Christine gets across the basics of ecological relationships. She emphasizes the need to protect all the plants and creatures, no matter how small and seemingly insignificant. The children even learn why the park does not disturb nature's balance by spraying to rid the islands of mosquitoes: The insects provide food for birds and other animals.

And we provide tasty nibbles for them, it seems. I had come prepared with a mosquito net face covering. "You're not allowed to wear that," one 11-year-old boy informed me. "You have to get bitten like the rest of us." He and his companions soon relented, however, deciding that the mosquitoes would get inside the netting and give me the required bloodletting they'd already endured. From about April to November, the insect population on the islands soars. I was awed by the number of mosquitoes, and this was only April. Then there are the tiny sand flies, the "no-see-ums," that attack in invisible waves.

To explore the mangrove zone, we cut across the island through the hammock, a slight rise covered with lush hardwoods, the names of which ring of the tropics: mahogany, gumbo-limbo, lignum vitae. The mosquitoes were winning by the time we emerged on the other shore, and we dashed into the shallow water. Christine offered several warnings: "Don't touch anything orange." Fire sponges and fire corals, for example, can deal nasty stings. And be careful of the sea anemones: "If it's bigger than a fist, it may hurt you with its sting." Sea urchins? "Touch softly. Don't touch hard, or they can prick your hand." Then, with the aid of glass-bottom buckets, we were examining everything. There were a lot of spiny lobsters—which have no claws— and they moved very fast. We soon caught on to their trick of swimming backward. Then we were able to examine them.

One child picked up a gnarled brown creature known as a sea cucumber. The kids squealed when it squirted out liquid. They squealed even more over a hermit crab, an enormous red one that emerged from its borrowed shell home. By now all kinds of fish were jumping as we slogged on through the water. "I caught a fish, I caught a fish, a little silver one!" came the cries. Any marine animals caught in examining nets were released after study.

Some years ago children were up to some less innocent gathering in another part of the park. The late Virginia Tannehill remembered the problems that came with drug trafficking in the 1970s and '80s. I visited her one afternoon on the seaward side of Elliott Key, where she had lived for some 22 years. She and one other island resident had life tenancy in the park. Her house and dock were ingeniously created out of driftwood and other flotsam and jetsam. "All the wood doors and the bar came off the *Mandalay* that sank out here," she said. "The big beams came from out in the mangrove." (That was before there was a park here; it's not legal to collect anything now.) She and her husband "started coming to Elliott in a little bitty boat, fishing," she explained. "We bought the land when we knew it wasn't going to be developed. We came over here to get away from development." The lively native Virginian was here when developers, knowing the area was to be declared a monument, at the eleventh hour gouged a 120-foot-wide track down the center of seven-mile-long Elliott Key. "We called it Spite Highway," she said.

The Tannehills helped to patrol the park. "At the beginning, when it first started coming in on the beach, I'd never seen marijuana. I thought it was hay or something. The Coast Guard said to just break it up on the beach. One time we'd religiously broken up five or six bales. And the next morning there was a big trawler going up and down, and then we heard voices. He had hired, this guy, kids—13- and 14-year-olds. They all had little plastic bags and were picking it up out of the seaweeds. And he paid these kids so much per bag."

*F*OR NOW, drug trafficking has slowed in the park. But other problems remain, ranging from Australian pines and other exotic groundlings that crowd out native vegetation to inept boaters. "Reef clowns," said Wayne Landrum. "Look at all the shallows." From atop the little lighthouse on Boca Chita Key, we looked down into transparent green waters—and great crisscrosses gouged in the white sand by boat propellers.

Richard Curry, resource manager for the park, later told me that prop scars last for years. Sometimes the grass beds—essential for water clarity and as nursery habitat—never grow back. "And how long does it take a coral reef to grow back?" he asked. "A lot of visitors here have not learned how to use a coral reef. You don't just drop an anchor into coral." The figures he cited are impressive, given that each anchoring tears up on average two to three square feet of bottom. "Say 1,000 boats are out on a weekend. Imagine 1,000 anchors, times 52 weeks. That means for the park 104,000 square feet, or about 2.4 acres of sea grass, torn up each year just from anchoring! Running aground tears up 15 to 20 square feet or more." The park has already installed mooring buoys in heavily visited areas, which may curtail damage.

A bigger question looms: water quality, upon which the health of the whole park depends. The week I arrived, a freighter had caught fire in the Straits of Florida, not far from the park. The Coast Guard doused the fire, towed the ship away, and sank it in 600 feet of water. The thought of what could happen if a major oil or toxic spill hit these reefs and mangroves worries many Floridians. On one T-shirt I saw emblazoned: "No Valdez in the Keys." Such disastrous incidents are not, however, the major threat here. The real problem comes with the growing numbers of people in south Florida: too much sewage, too much farm and industrial runoff, all pouring into these waters. That is the major worry for Richard Curry. High levels of ammonia are already leaching into the park from an adjacent landfill. Nearby Homestead Air Reserve Base has been declared an EPA Superfund site for heavy metals. "We are testing for water quality," Richard told me. Like canaries in a mine, tiny mycids, a kind of crustacean sensitive to elevated levels of toxins, are used to monitor the water.

Another simple colonial animal has a more positive role in maintaining water purity. If the tiny coral polyp and the red mangrove are chiefly builders here, the sponge is on cleanup detail. Sponges are the ultimate cleansers of the sea. They also form an important habitat for all sorts of creatures. In one large loggerhead sponge 16,000 small animals were recorded. Dr. James W. Porter, of the University of Georgia, has collaborated with the park in a study of the role of sponges.

"Sponges eat bacteria and other microorganisms," he notes. "The filter-feeding activity of sponges cleans the water. . . . we estimate that the present sponge population is capable of cleaning the entire water column of Biscayne Bay every two weeks." Without sponges, Porter says, "water clarity and water quality throughout the park would drop dramatically."

A conflict arose in the 1980s between ecologists and small-scale commercial spongers who fished these waters. After a blight hit Mediterranean sponges, the rate of harvest increased greatly. Spongers took only 4 of the more than 100 species, but these were the most abundant species. In 1991 sponging was entirely banned in the park.

Another problem, less easily addressed, has emerged in recent years. In the wake of increasing pressure from tourism, both on the land and in the water, I heard strong pleas for more protection of this fragile ecosystem. Reefs in adjacent John Pennekamp Coral Reef State Park have suffered severe damage in recent years, much of it attributed to the boats and diving activities of some one million visitors each year. Access for commercial boats carrying tourists is strictly limited in Biscayne National Park. These limitations rankle some visitors.

Others treasure this least touched corner of Florida's reef system. One diver said it best about this special place: "I like to have it and not be able to get to it easily, rather than not have it at all."

FOLLOWING PAGES: Pink shell palace—here camouflaged by algae—spells downfall for the queen conch. Prized for its lustrous shell and delicious flesh, the protected species has been seriously depleted in Florida.

STEPHEN FRINK

STEPHEN FRINK (ALL)

Reef-wrecked tramp steamer Alicia *lures a curious scuba diver and some brown chromis fish. Above, the diver hovers over the ribs of the ill-fated steamer, which piled onto Ajax Reef in 1905. "Wreckers"—licensed salvagers—swarmed* Alicia's *decks to grab a rich bounty of silks, laces, pianos, and liquors destined for Havana. Today numerous shipwrecks attract divers to these waters. The toothy challenge of a spotted moray (left) poses little threat. The fierce-looking eels rarely attack unless a hand pokes inadvertently into their crevice homes.*

Even in the gaudy realm of the coral reef, a brilliant queen angelfish stands out. Hundreds of fish species and other sea creatures find niches in the park's reef environment, which has been likened to a

rain forest in fragility and species diversity. A red fire coral behind the fish's tail causes burning irritation with its toxic cells. A sea fan (below) looks like an exotic underwater fern, but is formed by colonies of polyps.

Katmai
Kingdom of the Wild

By Kim Heacox
Photographs by Tom Bean

*H*ER EYES WERE DARK, her ears golden. Her furry face framed a nose that sniffed the forest with a keenness thousands of times greater than yours or mine. She stood on a trail with two cubs a year and a half old by her side. They wore the same on-guard posture as their mother: heads up, shoulders forward, senses focused on the spot where a lone intruder stood.

The threesome was a family of Alaskan brown bears; the intruder was me. I say intruder because bears live in Katmai National Park and Preserve, and I do not.

Like most visitors to Katmai, I had taken a jet from Anchorage 300 miles southwest to King Salmon, on the Alaska Peninsula, where park headquarters stand. From there I took a small floatplane to Brooks Camp, on the shore of Naknek Lake. En route, the pilot dipped a wing for better views of muskeg, tundra, lakes, swans, beaver dams, and a bull moose dwarfed by a wild, sweeping land that climbed into distant, shadowed mountains. As the land swept away, it carried me with it across Katmai National Park and Preserve—4.1 million acres of hope, where wilderness is a tonic for the human soul.

The plane touched down and taxied to shore, where a ranger waited to greet me and the others on board. We gathered in a log cabin that serves as a visitor center at Brooks Camp, between the lodge and a campground, and were briefed on the most important matter at hand: safety in bear country.

"Never run from a bear," the ranger said. "Running can elicit a chase response, and nobody in the wilderness can outrun a bear. Brooks Camp sits in the middle of critical brown bear habitat. Give them the right-of-way. If you encounter one, don't panic. Identify yourself, speak in a normal voice, wave your arms slowly. Back away diagonally if it comes toward you. But never run."

Ranger Frank Starr, based in a remote cabin on Katmai's Amalik Bay, supplements food supplies with fresh-caught salmon for lunch.

PRECEDING PAGES: Prime attraction at Katmai National Park, Alaskan brown bears comb Brooks Falls for salmon bucking upstream to spawn. Three cubs watch their mother expectantly from the bank.

KATMAI
NATIONAL PARK
AND PRESERVE

LOCATION: Alaska
ESTABLISHED: December 2, 1980
SIZE: 4,090,000 acres

Iliamna Lake

0   10   20 km
0   10   20 mi

Kukaklek Lake

Kamishak Bay

McNeil Cove

Battle Lake Cabins■

NATIONAL PRESERVE

ALAGNAK
WILD
RIVER

Nonvianuk
Camp ■
Nonvianuk Lake

Kulik Lodge
Kulik Lake

MCNEIL RIVER
STATE GAME
SANCTUARY

▲ Enchanted
Lake Lodge

American Creek

Oakley Peak +
4,625

+ Sugarloaf Mountain
2,085

Hammersly Lake

Lake
Coville

Murray Lake

Grosvenor
Lake Lodge ■

Lake
Grosvenor

■ Lake Camp
To King Salmon

Portage
Trail

Bay of
Islands

Naknek Lake   North Arm

Naknek

Savonoski
Wolverine
Falls

Kaguyak Crater•

Dumpling Mountain +...
2,440   ▲ Brooks Camp

Brooks Falls

Mount La Gorce +
3,183

Iliuk Arm

Rainbow

Hook Glacier

Devils Desk
+ 6,411   Ninagiak

Brooks Lake

Visitor Center

Mount Denison +
7,606

Kukak Volcano
6,700

Hallo
Bay

Mount Kelez +
3,250

Margot
Falls

Serpent Tongue
Glacier

Hallo Glacier

Kukak Bay

+ Granite Peak
1,683

Yori Pass

▲ Three Forks
Overlook ☂

Baked Mountain +
3,685

Mount Griggs +
7,600

+ Snowy Mountain
7,090

Katla
Bay

Novarupta +
4,860

Knife Creek
Glaciers

Katmai Pass•

+ Red Mountain
1,721

Angle Creek

+ Mount Katmai
6,715

Geographic
Harbor

Takayofo

Trident
Volcano
6,010

Mount Megeik +
7,250

Crater

Gertrude Peak +
1,141

Mount Martin +
6,050

Kinak Bay

BECHAROF NATIONAL
WILDLIFE REFUGE

KEJULIK MTS.

Takli

Amalik Bay

Kejulik Creek

Dakavak
Bay

Becharof
Lake

Kejulik

Katmai
Bay

Kashvik
Bay

SHELIKOF

Cape
Kubugakli

▲ Campground
🏃 Hiking Trail
– – – Unpaved Roads
•••••• Hiking Trails

Alinchak
Bay

TEN THOUSAND OF SMOKES

VALLEY OF

Ukak River

King Salmon River

And if you encounter three, what then? "Hey bear," I said clearly, standing my ground and waving my arms on the forest trail. "Hoooo beeeaaarrr...."

The mother stood up on her hind legs. Her cubs did the same. They were 150 feet away. Too close. Park regulations said I should have been at least twice that distance from a mother with young. But we had met in the cover of a thick forest, rather than along an open river or lakeshore, and now stood staring at each other with what probably amounted to a hundred centuries of accumulated suspicion and fear. I knew no bear was more dangerous than a mother with cubs. I also knew that, while some bears in the Brooks Camp area were relatively accustomed to people, others were more wary.

Katmai is home to an estimated 1,500 to 2,000 brown bears, the largest protected population in Alaska. The same species as grizzlies—*Ursus arctos*—brown bears live within a hundred miles of the coast. They eat more fish, which gives them a higher protein diet, and are therefore larger. While adult grizzlies in interior Alaska and elsewhere in the United States average only 300 to 600 pounds, male brown bears can exceed 1,000 pounds in the fall. Over the years they have been labeled dangerous and unpredictable, which they can be, yet seldom have they been called smart and resourceful, which they always are.

Let's turn the tables and consider ourselves. On meeting the great bear, we might fall to the ground in a protective fetal position or scream and run away. We might blow a whistle, climb a tree, or take a photograph. We might throw the bear food or shoot it dead. With behavior like that, clearly we, not the bears, are the unpredictable ones.

The mother bear and her cubs dropped back onto their forepaws and moved off the trail across a bed of moss, melting into the forest. As they went, the cubs glanced over their shoulders as if to make certain I wasn't following.

The trail took me deeper into the forest, then crested a small hill with a grassy clearing at its top, and arrived at a raised wooden platform at Brooks Falls on the Brooks River. A dozen people stood on the platform, among them Roslyn Rodeheaver, a park naturalist enjoying her fourth summer in Katmai. I scanned the river and counted eight bears, some of them young, some old, some above the falls, some below, all of them fishing for salmon.

"Between now and late in the fall, these bears may put on 40 percent of their body weight eating salmon," Roslyn told me. As she spoke, the salmon pooled below the six-foot-high falls, sometimes so thick they appeared to be one organism, a living river within a river— each preparing to surmount the final hurdle in the long journey back to the spawning grounds where they had emerged as fry three to five years earlier. They were sockeyes, also called red salmon, one of five species found in the Pacific, the others being king, silver, chum, and pink salmon.

*T*WO BEARS WAITED at the top of the falls in anticipation of the next fish that would jump within their reach. Most of the leaping salmon were off target, their speed and trajectory sending them head over tail into the white water. But I estimated every tenth jump was a good one, with the fish landing in the clear, swift water just above the falls, then streaking upstream to spawn, bring forth a new generation, and die. It was these fish, however— among the best jumpers in the river—that every so often landed in the waiting jaws of a bear.

Cheers rose from the platform when this happened, as the bear would stand for a moment with the salmon flopping in its teeth. Most bears retreated to the riverbank to eat the fish under cover of alders and spruce, but a few ate them where they caught them, on a rock in a rapid, in a riffle near shore, or sometimes deep in midcurrent, balancing on three paws while holding the fish with the fourth paw pressed against the opposite leg.

A hierarchy prevailed, with the oldest, largest males commanding the best spots. Diver, an old battle-scarred boar with a belly that nearly dragged on the ground, owned a part of the river known as the Jacuzzi—a pool below the falls where the water bubbled and the salmon gathered. He would wade in shoulder deep, plunge completely under, and surface 20 seconds later with a fish in his mouth. Then he would walk to a nearby island to eat his meal. Being so successful and well fed, he seldom ate an entire fish, but instead took a few bites out of the belly, then returned to the Jacuzzi to dive again, while screaming gulls and smaller bears descended on the half-eaten salmon floating downriver.

"Diver makes it look easier than it is," Roslyn said. "As cubs, these bears are unable to catch healthy fish, so they watch and learn from their mothers, and they often grow up using the same techniques. It takes both practice and patience." Her words rang true as we watched one young bear, probably a three-year-old in its first summer alone, lunging wildly for schools of salmon, slapping the water with its paws, and usually coming up empty.

So technique, size, and dominance all proved important to the bears' success in fishing. Excitement filled the viewing platform as we watched two bears compete for a fishing spot atop the falls. Rather than stand face to face, they squared off side to side—a behavior called posturing—growling and glaring not three feet apart. Suddenly a fight erupted, with flashing teeth and swinging paws. One bear was slightly larger and charged, forcing the other backward. The smaller bear put up a good fight, but was forced back again and fell over the falls and into the Jacuzzi. Diver looked up from his island where he was eating another salmon. The smaller bear surfaced, caught Diver's stare, and bolted out of the river, past the viewing platform, and into the forest.

We human beings felt invisible, for rarely would a bear look up at us on the platform, 12 feet above, and then only in what appeared to be a random glance or casual curiosity. Each bear seemed preoccupied with fishing and with the other bears around it. But experts would have recognized the telltale signs of stress caused by human presence: yawning, salivation, and an increased rate of those "random" glances. As the hours passed at Brooks Falls, I came to realize that beneath a surface tranquillity—the sound of tumbling water, the flight of swallows, the majesty of wild animals—there flowed an undercurrent of tension. The salmon, bears, and birds were absorbed in the serious business of survival.

For two incredible weeks that July, 42 million sockeye salmon would flood into Bristol Bay, a lower arm of the Bering Sea directly west of Katmai. "It is the richest sockeye salmon fishery in the world," said Jeff Regnart, a commercial fisheries biologist with Alaska's Department of Fish and Game, who works out of King Salmon.

The Bristol Bay sockeyes swarm up half a dozen major rivers, one of them the Naknek, which flows from Naknek Lake, the fourth largest lake in Alaska. Connecting Naknek Lake and smaller Brooks Lake is the mile-and-a-half-long Brooks River—a fish funnel that every July fills with salmon and attracts bears from surrounding areas and people from around the world. "This year," Jeff told me, "we estimate 3.6 million sockeyes went up the Naknek. That's a very strong run."

Strong indeed. In several one-minute segments at Brooks Falls I counted an average of a hundred leaping salmon. Sometimes six or eight fish would jump simultaneously, appearing to mesmerize the bears, which tried to pick one from the crowd and catch it.

From Jeff I would also learn that each spawning female sockeye produces 2,000 to 2,500 eggs. The fry emerge from lake or river gravel, spend one or two years in a lake, then swim down to sea as smolts. The greatest predation probably occurs in fresh water and in the first year of ocean life, with only 2 to 7 percent returning as adults.

Was it proper, then, I asked myself, to cheer for the bears catching fish, for the fish themselves, or for the wild beauty and fecundity of it all? Beyond surviving natural predation and disease, each sockeye below Brooks Falls had slipped past the drift nets of more than 1,800 commercial fishing boats in Bristol Bay, hundreds of nets set along the shore, and countless hooks and lines of sport fisherfolk in the Naknek River. Even from the viewing platform, I could see people downstream waist deep in the Brooks River, fishing.

Human beings have occupied the land around Brooks River for at least 4,000 years. They fished in the summers and perhaps wintered here as well. Partially reconstructed on a bluff on the opposite side of the river is a *barabara,* or Native American pit house, one of several in the area. Bears, too, have no doubt been here for many thousands of years, but exactly how long, and how many bears, is unknown. Records from decades ago when the lodge at Brooks Camp first opened indicate that bears were less numerous then, probably because people had historically driven them off and hunted them.

Today we are more sensitive, and the bears more numerous. As many as 25 bears visit Brooks Camp in July; more come in September and October, chiefly to feed on the dead and dying sockeye salmon that swam up Brooks River to spawn in July. Yet, to the delight of some people and the dismay of others, Brooks Camp on a sunny day in mid-July seems more like a wildlife theme park than a national park, looking as if all the tourists, bears, boats, planes, fish, and fishermen in Katmai had squeezed into one small area at the same time.

Rangers patrol the river daily, making announcements such as: "Everybody move out of the water and onto the far shore. We have a bear coming downstream." Fishermen and photographers are persuaded to gather on the riverbank, the bear floats past eating a salmon, the cameras whirr, and when the bear is far enough away the fishermen return to their sport. It is well orchestrated and appears harmless at first. But should it be that way? Should rangers load shotguns with cracker shells—as they do now—to frighten bears away from areas such as the lodge and cabins? And if that doesn't work, plastic bullets to sting them in the hind end?

From 1980 to 1990 the number of summer tourists visiting Katmai nearly quadrupled, jumping from 11,000 to 43,000, and the National Park Service became concerned that people were displacing bears; that Brooks Camp and the Brooks River, like so many other pristine places, were being loved to death.

Thus was born the Brooks River Area Development Concept Plan, its aim to determine whether more visitors could be accommodated "without overwhelming the natural and cultural resources by overuse or allowing the visitor experience to deteriorate because of overcrowding." Four alternatives were proposed, which varied from maintaining the status quo to removing Brooks Camp and eliminating fishing on the Brooks River. "Angling is the most intrusive human activity in this prime habitat," concluded a research report contained in the plan, "because it requires that the person be in the river in direct competition for space with foraging bears."

Standing back at the mouth of the river, where people were fishing shoulder to shoulder, I had wondered if salmon leaping and fighting with metal hooks in their mouths, then gently released, would have enough energy left to swim upstream to spawn. Should sport fishing be allowed in national parks? If so, what about sport hunting? And if not, what about berry picking? I wondered now, in a moment of self-analysis, if my earlier encounter with the mother bear and her cubs, causing them to detour through the forest, might have adversely affected them in some way. As I turned away from the crowded scene and walked down the trail past footprints, bear tracks, and a river filled with salmon, I wondered, too, if national parks, like hotels, shouldn't have a "No Vacancy" policy. For how many people can squeeze in before a park's essential wilderness—its very ambience—is forced out?

*I*N 1916 the National Park Service was created, and was directed to administer the national parks so as to "provide for the enjoyment of same in such manner and by such means as will leave them unimpaired for the enjoyment of future generations." This ambiguous, dichotomous mandate has been debated for decades, with development-minded people embracing the phrase "provide for the enjoyment" and preservation-minded people the phrase "leave them unimpaired."

"It is apparent," wrote Edward Abbey in *Desert Solitaire,* "that we cannot decide the question of development versus preservation by a simple referral to holy writ or an attempt to guess the intention of the founding fathers; we must make up our own minds and decide for ourselves what the national parks should be and what purpose they should serve." In Katmai, as in every other national park, preserve, and monument in Alaska, decisions made now will probably influence the land and its inhabitants for a long, long time.

Katmai National Park and Preserve, formerly a national monument, was created in 1980 when Jimmy Carter signed the Alaska National Interest Lands Conservation Act. Geographically, the park can be divided into three provinces: lake, mountain, and coast. The lake province, which contains Brooks Camp, lies to the west, where the terrain tumbles from high, treeless tundra into forest and finally into any of several large lakes: Naknek, Nonvianuk, Kulik, Coville, Grosvenor, Kukaklek, and Battle. Each lake is fed by rivers from the mountains and drained by rivers bound for Bristol Bay. *(Continued on page 186)*

*A*sh-strewn landscape surrounding a backpacker recalls the formation of the Valley of Ten Thousand Smokes. One of the most powerful volcanic eruptions of modern times racked Katmai in 1912. A fiery blizzard of ash and pumice blanketed the 40-square-mile valley. Steam wafting from hot vents in the volcanic tuff inspired the area's name. Its fires now cooled, the valley holds scenic wonders such as the Ukak River gorge (above), where the author watches the river rush through a narrow channel of eroded rock.

"*Naknek Lake is so spectacular it doesn't look real,*" *says angler Mark Emery of Katmai's largest body of fresh water. Mark acts as a fishing and photography guide. Naknek offers fishermen and campers deep-water coves sheltered by mountains and quiet islands thick with*

*alder. Rocky and weedy shoals teem with sport fish, such as the northern
pike on Mark's line. This stretch of water, the Bay of Islands, also lures
boaters who favor canoes and kayak-style boats—such as this one
drawn up at a lakeshore campsite—but sudden storms dictate caution.*

Boulder-studded tundra rises toward a small, unnamed lake south of Murray Lake. Here, above the timberline, clumps of alpine azalea lie close to the ground among the granite erratics. Frigid gales, shallow soil, and arid climate on Katmai's upper slopes restrict vegetation to hardy, low-growing species. Dwarf willow (below) and alpine azalea laced with branching reindeer moss (bottom) hug the spongy turf for warmth and shelter from the cutting wind.

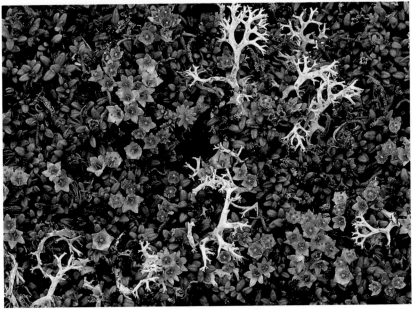

The mountains are part of the Aleutian Range, home to about 80 active volcanoes, several of which—Kukak, Kaguyak, Katmai, Trident, Megeik, and Martin—rise within the park. Over the mountains to the east lies the park coastline, on Shelikof Strait, opposite Kodiak Island, one of the wildest and least inhabited stretches of shore in all Alaska. This is the Katmai few people ever see, yet it is the one I know best, for it is here that my wife, Melanie, and I were stationed in the summer of 1985 as backcountry rangers.

Our job was to monitor wildlife and commercial fishermen, which we did when the weather allowed. Trollers and seiners from Kodiak and elsewhere would drop anchor near our small cabin and invite us for a dinner of Dungeness crab, embellished by stories about their years of fishing in these stormy waters off an unpeopled land. In a 15-foot Zodiak, Melanie and I patrolled more than 100 miles of wilderness coast. It twists and tumbles into bays, inlets, coves, and headlands where puffins, eagles, and sea lions live, and spreads into broad tidal flats and estuaries where bears dig for clams and wait for salmon.

On April 15, 1989, three weeks after the wreck of the *Exxon Valdez* in Prince William Sound, oil washed ashore on the Katmai coast, and Melanie and I returned as part of a task force to assess the damage. "The true loss is not one of dollars or individual birds or mammals," said the Park Service, "but in a radical and uncertain alteration of ecosystems whose integrity had been as uncompromised as any in America." It was a dirty, depressing job.

Now I would be making my third visit to the coast. The weather looked marginal as I climbed into a Cessna 206 floatplane with photographer Tom Bean and the pilot, Ed Dearwent, and we roared across Naknek Lake and lifted into the wind. Below us in the lake appeared the Bay of Islands, a scattering of vivid green on the blue water. As the topography climbed, so did we, flying over treeless ridges capped with snowfields. On the snow stood a herd of caribou, probably attracted to this cold, windy spot because there they might gain some relief from insects. Biologists have watched caribou, twitching under a cloud of mosquitoes or botflies, run up onto a ridge or snowfield to rid themselves of the pests. The temperature drop is too severe for the insects to tolerate. We circled the caribou and continued north to Kulik Lake, where Katmai National Park meets Katmai National Preserve. There we spent the night at Kulik Lodge.

The next day we turned east and threaded our way into the mountains. Peaks towered next to us, cliffs climbed off our wingtips, and rivers ran far below. I glanced at Ed to see if he, like me, was feeling nervous. But he looked completely unaffected, perhaps because he had 13,000 hours of flying under his belt, most of them in small planes in Alaska. We shot through a pass and dropped into the McNeil River drainage, on the northern boundary of the park. Winds buffeted the plane as we rounded Cape Douglas, southbound down the coast. Rain squalls loomed ahead, clouds surrounded us, and Ed finally turned the plane toward home, reciting a familiar flyer's adage: "There are old pilots and bold pilots," he said, "but no old, bold pilots."

As we approached Brooks Camp, flying back over Naknek Lake, the green and blue outside one window suddenly yawned into a huge, forbidding valley filled with ash and sliced by tumbling, turbid rivers; a netherworld one early explorer called "an abomination of desolation," and another, "the Valley of Ten Thousand Smokes." The second name stuck, but the first probably describes better the scene as it appeared on June 6, 1912. For on that date, the greatest volcanic eruption of the 20th century rocked the earth in a blast ten times more powerful than the 1980 explosion of Mount St. Helens.

"MY DEAR WIFE TANIA," wrote Ivan Orloff on June 9, 1912, from a fishing camp in Kaflia Bay on the Katmai coast. "First of all I will let you know of our unlucky voyage. I do not know whether we shall be either alive or well. . . . A mountain has burst near here, so that we are covered with ashes, in some places 10 feet and 6 feet deep. All this began on the 6th of June. Night and day we light lamps. We cannot see the daylight. In a word it is terrible, and we are expecting death at any moment, and we have no water. All the rivers are covered with ashes. Just ashes mixed with water. Here are darkness and hell, thunder and noise. . . . Vanka will tell you all about it. So kissing and blessing you both, good-bye. Forgive me. Perhaps we shall see each other again. God is merciful. Pray for us." He signed the letter, then added, "The earth is trembling; it lightens every minute. It is terrible. We are praying." Orloff apparently survived the ordeal.

Ash circled the world and temperatures dropped. Acid rain singed linen off clotheslines in Vancouver, British Columbia, more than a thousand miles away. On Kodiak Island, just across the Shelikof Strait from Mount Katmai, ash fell a foot deep, and lanterns held at arm's length at midday could not be seen. One journal entry from Cold Bay read: "They report the top of Katma Mountain blun of. There was a lot of Pummy stone in their dory when they got here and the say Hot Rock was flying all eraund them."

Four years later, on July 31, 1916, a National Geographic Society expedition, under the leadership of Robert F. Griggs, ascended Katmai Pass and beheld the unbelievable. Griggs wrote: "The sight that flashed into view as we surmounted the hillock was one of the most amazing visions ever beheld by mortal eye. The whole valley as far as the eye could reach was full of hundreds, no thousands—literally tens of thousands—of smokes curling up from its fissured floor. From our position they looked as small as the little fumaroles near by, but realizing something of their distance we knew many of them must be gigantic. Some were sending up columns of steam which rose a thousand feet before dissolving."

Here was a place, Griggs thought as he lay awake that night, every bit as remarkable as Yellowstone, one that surely belonged in the pantheon of America's great national parks and monuments. Two years later, in 1918, Katmai National Monument was created. Griggs returned to the Valley of Ten Thousand Smokes twice more—in 1917 and 1919—each time leading a National Geographic Society expedition. The members conducted detailed studies into the nature of volcanism, while camping in the valley and cooking their bacon and flapjacks over hot steam vents.

Upon discovering that the summit of Mount Katmai was a deep, steep-walled, lake-filled caldera, Griggs concluded that this had been the outlet for the great eruption of 1912. He was wrong. In 1953 scientists determined that Novarupta, a volcanic vent five miles from Mount Katmai, was the true source of the eruption; that as Novarupta had shot skyward, the summit of Mount Katmai, connected to the same volcanic plumbing, had collapsed, forming a caldera.

Four cubic miles of molten rock burst from Novarupta, and with it an even greater volume of frothy pumice and ash mixed with hot, incandescent gases.

"*T*HE VOLUME OF pumice and ash rushing out of the vent was so great that not all of it could get airborne," wrote volcanologist Judy Fierstein in her book *The Valley of Ten Thousand Smokes*. "A flood of pumice rushed from the choked vent and actually flowed as a dense, tumbling mixture of pumice blocks, fine ash, and hot gas that moved down the former Ukak River valley to form the nearly flat-surfaced valley we see today."

Thus this section of the Ukak River Valley, once rich with spruce forest, muskeg, beaver ponds, and moose, was buried beneath hundreds of feet of compacted ash, creating the present Valley of Ten Thousand Smokes. Katmai Pass, on a once much traveled trading route between the Gulf of Alaska and the Bering Sea, was the portal through which Robert Griggs made his remarkable discovery.

Even without active volcanism, the valley is still mesmerizing. Winds can blow 115 miles an hour, picking up great clouds of ash that fill the eyes and ears, and sometimes knocking hikers off their feet. Rains can fall for days, swelling the River Lethe, named for the mythological river of forgetfulness, and occasionally sweeping hikers to their deaths. And clouds can roll in so thick and low as to completely disorient a capable backcountry traveler. So why go there? Because there is no other landscape like it, and when the weather smiles in a calm prism of summer air, when twilight paints a palette of amber, ocher, and cinnabar and a full moon rises above the snowy summit of Mount Griggs, it is truly a wonderland.

So it was when photographer Tom Bean, his wife, Susan, and I traveled by bus on a 23-mile road from Brooks Camp to the Valley of Ten Thousand Smokes, hoisted our packs, and hiked into the volcanic heart of Katmai. We bent to admire flowering poppies, crossed the River Lethe with water to our thighs, then sweated up a slope of cinders and ash to the Baked Mountain Cabin. The fog rolled in that night, and we huddled in our bunks, reading the cabin logbook that records impressions and experiences of visitors to the valley.

The next morning we hiked toward Novarupta, only two miles away. The fog played tricks on us, and we began to question our navigation, when suddenly it cleared and before us towered the dark lava dome, 200 feet high, a quarter mile across, and still steaming. Ferns and wildflowers grew around the warm vents, and we got down on our knees for a better look, warming our hands in the steam.

After lunch, Tom and Susan went one way and I went another, with plans to rendezvous that night back at Baked Mountain Cabin. I rationed my water and hiked for hours, enjoying a glorious, windless day in a land seldom so kind. Climbing high above Katmai Pass, I could see the blue expanse of Shelikof Strait far below, and in the misty distance beyond it, Kodiak Island. Mount Megeik loomed above me, with its glaciers glistening and summit steaming, and I stood alone, cradled in fire and ice, staring into a valley that had stunned Robert Griggs 75 years ago. Though the smokes are gone, the landscape is still breathtaking, and I sat in the sunshine a little stunned myself.

Heading back across the open valley and feeling as though I were the only living thing for miles, I came upon fresh bear tracks, one large set and two small. Could they be those of the mother and twin cubs I had encountered in the forest near Brooks Camp a few days ago and 35 miles away? My heart raced. It was eleven o'clock at night; dusk had fallen, and the bears could be anywhere. The valley was alive. I hiked like the wind, looking over my shoulder, and arrived back at the Baked Mountain Cabin in darkness past midnight.

Tom and Susan were asleep. I grabbed the cabin journal, stepped outside with a flashlight, and wrote my own entry: "To the bears and volcanoes of Katmai, and the unpredictability of both; that we who can alter any landscape in the world will have the wisdom to leave this one alone."

FOLLOWING PAGES: Near Takayofo Creek in the watershed terrain of southwestern Katmai, caribou migrating across the tundra graze on their favorite foods, lichens and grasses.

FRED HIRSCHMANN

ROLLIE OSTERMICK

Snowy head plumage gleaming, a bald eagle perches on the snag of a dead tree near Katmai's Brooks Camp. Another guards a nest (opposite, upper left) atop an arch of alder on a basalt cliff in Geographic Harbor. Bald eagles thrive in the park. Fish-eaters, they stay close to the seacoast, lakes, and rivers, ever ready to snatch fish from the surface or scavenge carcasses on shore.

*F*orested headlands (below) reach into Kukak Bay on Katmai's rugged seacoast. Bays such as Kukak and Amalik, where a salmon seiner rides at anchor (right), shelter fishing boats in stormy weather. In 1991 Alaska's commercial fishermen netted a catch valued at about 1.1 billion dollars, a third of it salmon. Beyond Kukak Bay, a glimpse of icy peaks bares the heart of this wilderness park— a shimmering realm of volcanoes and glaciers.

NOTES ON CONTRIBUTORS _____

TOM BEAN, free-lance photographer and former park ranger in Alaska, needed his backcountry experience to photograph the wild landscapes of Katmai. Tom lives near Flagstaff, Arizona, and has photographed for numerous Society publications.

A 1983 Pulitzer Prize winner for feature photography and Gold Medalist in the World Press Photo Foundation competition, free-lancer JAY DICKMAN is based in Littleton, Colorado. He has worked on several assignments for NATIONAL GEOGRAPHIC.

SEYMOUR L. FISHBEIN, during his 25 years as a staff member, wrote and edited many stories about parks and his abiding passion, canoeing. Since retirement in 1987, he has written two Special Publications: *Yellowstone Country* and *Grand Canyon Country.*

Widely published free-lancer STEPHEN FRINK specializes in underwater photography. He knows Biscayne intimately, being located right next door in Key Largo, Florida. His photographs have appeared in many magazines and Society publications.

Free-lance writer KIM HEACOX won the Lowell Thomas Award for excellence in travel journalism in 1987 and 1990. Recent books include *Iditarod Spirit* and *In Denali.* A 12-year Alaska resident, Kim lives just outside Denali National Park and says he always enjoys writing about his adopted home state.

MICHAEL MELFORD's photographs have appeared on the covers of *Life, Newsweek, Holiday,* and other magazines. A free-lancer, he lives on a farm in Mount Kisco, New York, and has undertaken assignments for TRAVELER and for several Special Publications.

Staff member since 1971, TOM MELHAM has written for NATIONAL GEOGRAPHIC and for many Special Publications. His diving skills enabled him to explore the underwater world off California's Channel Islands. Long accustomed to writing about American parks, he found this one unlike any other.

RICHARD OLSENIUS, a 12-year veteran of the *Minneapolis Tribune,* became a free-lance photographer in 1981. He also writes books and composes music. His photographs have appeared in Special Publications and in NATIONAL GEOGRAPHIC articles.

Longtime staff member CYNTHIA RUSS RAMSAY has written chapters for many Special Publications. An avid skier, she thrives in the snow and high country. Hiking and climbing in North Cascades park in Washington State brought her new challenges and a sense of the grandeur of this mountain wilderness.

A free-lance photojournalist based in the Seattle area, Washington, PHIL SCHOFIELD has covered the American West for 20 years. His assignments for Society publications include an award-winning story on sagebrush country for NATIONAL GEOGRAPHIC.

Associated with the Black Star photo agency, JAMES A. SUGAR has free-lanced as a writer and photographer for NATIONAL GEOGRAPHIC since 1969 and has photographed for several Special Publications.

MEDFORD TAYLOR lives on the Chesapeake Bay in Maryland and has worked on five continents as a photojournalist since 1969. His photographs have appeared in several Special Publications and in NATIONAL GEOGRAPHIC and TRAVELER.

A free-lance writer living in Flagstaff, Arizona, SCOTT THYBONY has carried out Society assignments from Michigan to Mexico. His background in anthropology and his enthusiasm for the open country of the Southwest added perception to his story about the Guadalupe Mountains in Texas.

Staff member since 1971, JENNIFER C. URQUHART has explored many U. S. parks on field trips for articles in TRAVELER and chapters in Special Publications. She found her two chapter assignments—which took her from horseback riding in North Dakota to snorkeling in Florida—refreshingly different.

NORBERT WU's writing, photography, and cinematography of marine life have appeared in hundreds of magazines, books, and films. Among his books are *Life in the Oceans* and *Beneath the Waves.* A free-lancer, he is based in Orinda, California.

ACKNOWLEDGMENTS _____

The Book Division is especially grateful for the assistance given by National Park Service superintendents and staff of these little-known parks and by the people named or quoted in the text. We also wish to thank the following: Frederick M. Bayer, Diane Devine, Peter Howorth, Jennifer Hunt, Sir Lancelot Jones, Lyndal L. Laughrin, Therese Madoui, Russell H. Niedhauk, Karen Semerau, Tom and Lorraine Tescher, and George E. Watson.

ADDITIONAL READING _____

The reader may wish to consult the *National Geographic Index* for related articles and books, in particular *National Geographic's Guide to the National Parks of the United States.* National Park Service handbooks and the KC Publications' park series *The Story Behind the Scenery* may also prove useful, as well as the following books. North Cascades: Fred Beckey, *Challenge of the North Cascades;* Susan Schwartz, *Cascade Companion.* Voyageurs: Grace Lee Nute, *The Voyageur;* Robert Treuer, *Voyageur Country.* Theodore Roosevelt: David McCullough, *Mornings on Horseback;* Tom McHugh, *The Time of the Buffalo.* Channel Islands: Adelaide L. Diran, *Pieces of Eight Channel Islands;* Karen J. Dowty, *The California Channel Islands.* Guadalupe Mountains: David F. Costello, *The Desert World;* Alan Tennant, *The Guadalupe Mountains of Texas.* Biscayne: Rachel Carson, *The Edge of the Sea;* Gilbert L. Voss, *Coral Reefs of Florida.* Katmai: Dave Bohn, *Rambles Through an Alaskan Wild: Katmai and the Valley of the Smokes;* Wilson F. Erskine, *Katmai.*

Index

Boldface indicates illustrations.

Abbey, Edward 179
Achenbach Hills, Theodore
  Roosevelt NP, N. Dak.:
  homestead ruins **88-89**
Adams Key, Biscayne NP, Fla. 154,
  154, 160-161
Agaves 125, **129**
Alaska *see* Katmai NP and Preserve
Alaska National Interest Lands
  Conservation Act (1980) 179
Algae: marine 148, 152, **164-165,**
  kelp 96, **116, 117;** watermelon
  snow 19
Amalik Bay, Katmai NP, Alas.:
  fishing boat **195;** ranger **173**
Anacapa Island, Channel Islands
  NP, Calif. **92-93,** 96-97;
  wildflowers **100**
Anemone, rose **95**
Angelfish, queen **168**
Apache Indians: Guadalupe
  Mountains 125, 134, 137
Azalea, alpine **184, 185**

Backpacking: Guadalupe
  Mountains 122-127, 134-137;
  North Cascades NP **20, 21, 32;**
  Voyageurs NP 57-59
Badlands: Theodore Roosevelt NP
  4-5, 66-67, 68, **76-77,** 82-83, 84,
  90-91, geology 75, 82, 83, 90-91
Bald eagles 56, 57, **192, 193**
Bartlett, John 120, 122
Bears: Alaskan brown **6-7, 170-**
  171, 172, 175-179, 189; black **40,**
  47
Belcher, Robert 135
Biscayne NP, Fla. **146-169;** at-a-
  glance 200; boating 150, 152,
  156, 158, 159, **159,** reef damage
  162, 163; development
  pressures 150, 152, 162; ecology
  152, 153, 154, 156, 160, 161;
  education program 154, **154,**
  160-161; mangroves 153, **154-**
  155, 156, **156-157,** 160, 161;
  map **151;** snorkelers **1, 146,**
  158, 159; water quality 152, 156,
  160, 162-163; wreck diving **166,**
  167
Bison 68, 71, 72-73, **80-81,** 84, 85
Boating: Biscayne NP 150, **156,**
  162, 163, glass-bottom boats
  152, **158,** 159, **159;** Voyageurs
  NP 43, 47, **49;** *see also* Canoeing
Boise Cascade Corporation 44, 46,
  58
Boston Basin, North Cascades NP,

Wash. **9;** cliffs above 13, **22-23**
Bremen, Gary 160
Bristol Bay, Alas.: salmon runs 177
Brooks Camp, Katmai NP, Alas.
  172, 175, 178, 179
Brooks Falls, Katmai NP, Alas.:
  bears **6-7, 170, 171,** 172, 175-
  179; salmon runs 176-178;
  tourist management 178-179
Buffalo Soldiers 134
Bush, Kelly 29
Butterfield Overland Mail Line:
  station ruin **131**

Cactuses: cholla **128-129;** claret
  cup **129;** prickly pear **100**
Caire, Justinian 98
California *see* Channel Islands NP
Canoeing: Voyageurs NP **38,** 41-48,
  48, 56, 57, 65
Caribou 59, 186, **190-191**
Carson, Rachel 152
Cascade Pass, North Cascades NP,
  Wash. 27
Cascade Range, U. S.-Canada *see*
  North Cascades NP
Cedars, western red 14, 34, **34-35**
Challenger Glacier, North
  Cascades NP, Wash. **30-31**
Channel Islands National Marine
  Sanctuary, Calif. 96
Channel Islands NP, Calif. **92-117;**
  at-a-glance 200; boat access 96,
  101, 110; Chumash Indians 96,
  108; diving 96-97, **117;** ecology
  98-99, 111; fishing 96; hiking
  106, 109, 110; kelp forests 96-97,
  116, 117; map **97;** pinnipeds
  109, 110-111, **112-113, 114;**
  ranching 99, 103, 107, 108;
  shipwrecks **104-105,** 108
Chelan, Lake, Wash. 14, 28
Chihuahuan Desert, Mexico-U. S.
  122, **128-129;** gypsum dunes
  135, **138-139**
Chipmunk **24**
Cholla, walkingstick **128-129**
Chromis, brown **166**
Chumash Indians 96, 108
Clary, Ben 43
Columbine, Sitka **33**
Columbus, Christopher 153
Conch, queen **164-165**
Condominius giganticus 153
Coral reefs *see* Biscayne NP
Coreopsis, giant **100,** 109
Cornell, Ted 74
Cosley, Kathy 19, 26, 27

Counts, Helen 29
Courtney, Clifford 28-29
Courtney, Curt 29
Curry, Richard 162, 163

Davidson, Ed 153, **158**
Dearwent, Ed 186, 187
Deer: brainworms 59
Delong, Robert 110
de Mores, Marquis 73-74; ranch
  78, 79

Earnst, John 14
Eel: spotted moray **167**
Eiseley, Loren 136
El Capitan (promontory),
  Guadalupe Mountains NP **119,**
  120, 144, **144-145**
Elk 108, 134
Elkhorn Ranch, Theodore
  Roosevelt NP, N. Dak. 71, 72, 73,
  85
Elliott Key, Biscayne NP, Fla. 150,
  161-162
Emery, Mark **182**
Exxon Valdez oil spill (1989) 186

Falcon, prairie **77**
Fascell, Dante B. 150, 152
Fierstein, Judy 188
Fisher Creek Trail, North Cascades
  NP, Wash. 16-19
Fishing: Alaska 177, 178-179, 182-
  183, 194, boat **195,** guide **182,**
  183; Channel Islands 96;
  Voyageurs NP 42, 43, 50, fish
  contamination 50, 57, from
  floatplane **52-53,** guide **50, 51,**
  ice fishing **65**
Florida *see* Biscayne NP
Florida Keys National Marine
  Sanctuary, Fla. 152
Foxes, island 99, **107**
Freeman, Myron 74-75
Frijole Ranch, Guadalupe
  Mountains NP, Tex. 126
Fur traders *see* Voyageurs

Garibaldi (fish) **116**
Geographic Harbor, Katmai NP,
  Alas.: basalt cliff **193**
Gilmore, Ben and Isobel 136
Glaciers: North Cascades NP
  10-11, 17, 18, 19, **23,** 26, **30-31**
Gold rush: Voyageurs region 44
Grierson, Benjamin H. 143
Griggs, Robert F. 187-188
Grim, Lee 44-45, 57, 58, 59

Grizzly bears *see* Bears: Alaskan brown
Groundsels **12**
Guadalupe Mountains NP, Tex. **118-145**; at-a-glance 200; backpacking 122-127, 134-137; geology 120, 124-125, 135, 140-141, 144, **144**; map **122-123**; ranches 125-126, **130-131**, 135-136; winds 120, 122, 126, 135, 136, 137
Gypsum dunes 135, **138-139**

Hart, Pete 85
Hartmann, Glenna **103**
Heinselman, Bud and Fran 59
Heiser, John 73
Hemlocks: mountain 17; western 14
Herons: great blue, white phase **149**; tricolor **157**
Hiking: Channel Islands NP **106**, 109, 110; Guadalupe Mountains NP 122-127, 134-137; North Cascades NP 14, 16-19, **20, 21**, 27, 29, **32, 35**; Voyageurs NP 57-59
Horseback riding: Theodore Roosevelt NP **66-67**, 83, 84-85, **88**
Horses, wild **80**, 81
Hugar, Elbys 137
Hummingbird, black-chinned **133**
Hunter, J. C. 125-126, 134
Hunter Peak, Guadalupe Mountains NP, Tex. **128-129**

Ice fishing **65**
Ice plant 109
Ice worms 26
Islandia (development), Biscayne Bay, Fla. 152

Jays, scrub: Santa Cruz 99

Kabetogama Peninsula, Voyageurs NP, Minn. 43, 47, 56-59
Kallemeyn, Larry 46, 57
Katmai, Mount, Alas.: caldera 188
Katmai NP and Preserve, Alas. **170-195**; at-a-glance 200; bears **6-7, 170, 171**, 172, 175-179; fishing 178-179, 182, **182**, 183; map **174-175**; tourist management 178-179; *see also* Valley of Ten Thousand Smokes

Kaye, Bruce 73, 82, 85
Kellogg family: Esther 41, 43-44; Joe 43, 47, **48**; Martin 43-44, 47, **48**, 56, 57
Kelp: Channel Islands 96, **116, 117**
Kettle Falls Hotel, Voyageurs NP, Minn. 46-47
Kincaid, Jack 126
Kincaid, Noel 126, 137
Klemetsrud, Mark **78**
Kuehn, David 82, 83
Kukak Bay, Katmai NP, Alas. **194-195**

Lake Chelan NRA, Wash. 27-29; map **15**; waterfall **25**
Landrum, L. Wayne 150, 162
Lignite 75; underground fires 82
Lilies: Columbia **33**; glacier **23**
Little Missouri River, U. S. **66-67**, 82, **90-91**
Longhorn cattle 72, **90**, 99, 108
Loons: Voyageurs NP 46, **54**
Lynch, Jim 135

McKenney, Thomas L. 45
McKittrick Canyon, Guadalupe Mountains NP, Tex. 122, **142-143**; creek 124, **140**; geology 124-125, 140-141, reef trail **140-141**; pictograph **143**
Madrones, Texas **132, 133**
Maki, Mike 109
Maltese Cross Cabin, Theodore Roosevelt NP, N. Dak. 78, **78-79**
Mangroves: Biscayne NP 153, **154-155**, 156, **156-157**, 160, 161
Maple, bigtooth **140**
Maps: Biscayne NP **151**; Channel Islands NP **97**; Guadalupe Mountains NP **122-123**; Katmai NP **174-175**; North Cascades NP **15**; Theodore Roosevelt NP **70**; Voyageurs NP **42-43**
Marijuana trafficking 162
Marmot, hoary **33**
Martine, Evelyn 125, 137
Meadowlark, western **88**
Medora, N. Dak. 72, 73-74
Melin, Sharon 110-111
Mercury-contaminated fish: Voyageurs NP 50, 57
Mescal 125
Mice, deer: Channel Islands 99
Miller, Joe and Margaret 27
Minnesota *see* Voyageurs NP
Monkey flowers **12**
Moose: Voyageurs NP **55**

Morris, Don 108
Mountain climbing: North Cascades NP 18, 19, **22**, 23, 26-27, **30**
Mountain lion **121**

Naknek Lake, Alas. 177, 182-183, **182-183**
National Geographic Society: expeditions to Valley of Ten Thousand Smokes (1916-1919) 187-188
National Park System: mission 179; overcrowding 8, 178-179
The Nature Conservancy: Channel Islands reserve 98-99, **103**, 108
North Cascades Highway, Wash. 13, 24
North Cascades Institute 14
North Cascades NP, Wash. **10-37**; at-a-glance 200; fog 26-27; glaciers **10-11**, 17, 18, 19, **23**, 26, **30-31**; hiking 14, 16-19, **20, 21**, 27, 29, **32, 35**; map **15**; mountaineering 18, 19, **22**, 23, 26-27, **30**; prehistoric Indians 27; weather 14, 16, 18, 26-27, 34
North Dakota *see* Theodore Roosevelt NP
Novarupta (volcano), Alas. 189; 1912 eruption 188

Oberholtzer, Ernest 56
Ohlsten, Jim 27
Olson, Sigurd 56, 59
Oveson, Laverne **50, 51**
Oveson, Lucille **51**
Owen, Wally 83-84
Owls, great gray **35**
Oysters 153, 156

Painted Canyon, Theodore Roosevelt NP, N. Dak. **76-77**
Peaceful Valley Ranch, Theodore Roosevelt NP, N. Dak. 83
Pelicans: brown 57; white 44, 57
Peña, Mary 137
Peterson, Joanne 43, 44, 45, 46, **48**
Picket Range, North Cascades NP, Wash. **36-37**
Pictograph **143**
Picture Lake, North Cascades NP, Wash. **10-11**
Pinedrops **20**
Porcupine **35**
Porter, James W. 163
Prairie 74-75, **86-87, 89**

Prairie dogs **81**, 83-84
Pratt, Wallace E. 124

Quartz **54**

Rafting: Ross Lake NRA **24**
Rainbow Falls, Lake Chelan NRA, Wash. **25**
Rainy Lake, Voyageurs NP, Minn. 44-45, 59, **60-61;** quartz deposit **54;** water levels 46
Raleigh, Sir Walter 153
Rattlesnake, northern blacktail **129**
Rays, bat 97
Redoubt, Mount, North Cascades NP, Wash. **32**
Reef Rover IV (glass-bottom boat) 152, **158**, 159, **159**
Regnart, Jeff 177
Reindeer moss **185**
Reisch, Roger 127
Rodeheaver, Roslyn 175, 176
Rogers, Christine 161
Roosevelt, Theodore 77; bison hunting 68, 71; ranches 71, 72, 73, 84, 85, brand **78**, cabin **78-79**
Rosacker, Mark 125
Ross Lake NRA, Wash.: map **15;** rafting **24**

Sagebrush 75
Salmon: Alaska 194, fishing boat **195**, salmon runs **7**, 176-179
San Miguel (island), Channel Islands NP, Calif. 108-111, **114-115;** boating 110; bombing range 109; hiking 109, 110; pinnipeds 109, 110-111, **112-113**, **114;** plants 109
Sand dunes, gypsum 135, **138-139**
Santa Cruz (island), Channel Islands, Calif. **102-103;** feral animals 99; native animals 99; Nature Conservancy reserve 98-99, **103**, 108; ranching 99, 103, 108; rare plants 98-99
Santa Rosa (island), Channel Islands NP, Calif. **104-105**, **106-107;** biking 107; Chumash Indians 108; hikers **106;** island fox **107;** ranching 107, 108; shipwrecks **104-105**, 108; sport hunting 108; visitor permits 107
Scuba diving: Biscayne NP **166**, **167;** Channel Islands 96-97, **117**
Sea lions, California 109, 110-111, **112-113**

Sea urchin **116**
Seals, elephant: San Miguel 109, 111, **114**
Seliga, Joe 44
Sharkfin Tower, North Cascades NP, Wash.: mountaineers **22**
Shaver, C. Mack 94, 111
Shelikof Strait, Alas. 186
Shipwrecks: *Alicia* **166**, **167;** *Chickasaw* **104-105;** *Dora Bluhm* 108; *Mandalay* 162
Shuksan, Mount, Wash. **10-11**, 19, 26-27
Skagit River, B.C.-Wash.: rapids **24;** reservoirs 14
Skiing, cross-country 47, 56
Snail, turban **116**
Snorkelers **1**, **146**, **158**, **159**
Snowmobiles: Voyageurs NP 56
Snowshoeing **64**
Snyker, Jerry 47
Sparrows, white-throated 45
Sponges: water purifying role 163
Stanton, Carey 98
Stanton, Edwin L. 98
Star, bat **95**
Starr, Frank **173**
Stehekin River, Wash.: waterfall **25**
Stehekin Valley, Wash. 27-29
Stehekin Valley Ranch, Wash. 28
Sulentich, Jim 98-99
Sulfide Glacier, North Cascades NP, Wash. 19, 26
Sully, Alfred 82
Sunflowers **69**, 82

Tannehill, Virginia 161-162
Texas *see* Guadalupe Mountains NP
Theodore Roosevelt NP, N. Dak. **66-91;** at-a-glance 200; badlands **4-5**, **66-67**, 75, **76-77**, 82-83,

90-91, **90-91;** bison 72-73, **80-81**, 81, 84, 85; Elkhorn Ranch 71, 72, 73, 85; map **70;** prairie 74-75, **86-87**, **89;** prehistoric Indians 83
Thunder Creek Trail, North Cascades NP, Wash. 14, 16, **20**

Ukak River, Alas. **181**, 188

Valentine, Mary 109
Valley of Ten Thousand Smokes, Katmai NP, Alas. **180-181;** hiking 188-189; National Geographic Society expeditions (1916-1919) 187-188; volcanic eruption (1912) 181, 187, 188; weather 188-189
Voyageurs 42, 43, 45, 56, 57, 65
Voyageurs NP, Minn. **38-65;** at-a-glance 200; backpacking 57-59; canoeing **38**, 41-48, **48**, 56, 57, 65; fishing 42, 43, 50, **50**, **52-53**, 57, **65;** flies 46; geology 45, 54-55, 59; hotel 46-47; logging 42, 58, 59; map **42-43;** water pollution 50, 57; weather 45, 47; winter sports 47, 56, 64, **64**, **65;** wolves 59
Voyageurs Region National Park Association 47, 56

Weisberg, Saul 14, 16, 17, 18, 19, **20**, **21**
Whatcom Peak, North Cascades NP, Wash. **31**
Williams, Dolph: ranch **130-131**, 135-136
Willow, dwarf **185**
Wolves: Voyageurs NP 59

Yucca, soapweed **128-129**

Library of Congress ℭℙ Data

America's hidden treasures : exploring our little-known national parks / prepared by the Book Division, National Geographic Society.
    p. cm.
    Includes index.
    ISBN 0-87044-863-3
    1. National parks and reserves—United States. 2. United States—Description and travel—1981– I. National Geographic Society (U.S.). Book Division.
    E160.A577 1992
    917.304'928—dc20   92-12426
                                                ℭℙ

Composition for this book by the Typographic section of National Geographic Production Services, Pre-Press Division. Set in Garamond Light. Printed and bound by R. R. Donnelley & Sons, Willard, Ohio. Color separations by Graphic Art Service, Inc., Nashville, Tenn.; Lanman Progressive Co., Washington, D.C.; Lincoln Graphics, Inc., Cherry Hill, N.J.; NEC, Inc., Nashville, Tenn.; and Phototype Color Graphics, Pennsauken, N.J.

PARKS AT A GLANCE

- ## NORTH CASCADES NP
2105 State Route 20
Sedro Woolley, WA 98284
(360) 856-5700

Remote alpine peaks dappled with some 320 glaciers and deep, forested valleys. Western slopes moist; eastern, drier, sunnier. Wild, rugged terrain challenges mountain climbers. Abundant lakes, streams, and waterfalls lure hikers, campers, trail riders, boaters, fishermen. Permits needed for backcountry camping. Horses, charter planes, guides, and lodgings available in nearby communities. Snow may close lower valley roads and trails mid-October to April. Map, page 15.

- ## VOYAGEURS NP
3131 Highway 53
International Falls, MN 56649
(218) 283-9821

Forested lake country combines history with wilderness experience in this boaters' park. Four large, glacier-carved lakes and 26 smaller ones dotted with more than 900 islands form part of a 3,000-mile route paddled by French-Canadian voyagers. Rental motorboats, houseboats, and canoes available for groups and families May through October. Visitor centers, naturalist-guided boat tours, wildlife viewing. Several hundred island campsites; lodgings and resorts nearby. Winter activities include cross-country skiing, snowmobiling, ice fishing, snowshoeing, and winter camping. Map, pages 42-3.

- ## THEODORE ROOSEVELT NP
P.O. Box 7
Medora, ND 58645
(701) 623-4466

Scenic badlands along the Little Missouri River include two park units and the site of Roosevelt's Elkhorn Ranch. Park is open year-round, but parts may be closed in winter. Scenic drives; hiking and horseback trails. Entrance fee; picnic sites; campgrounds; permits required for backcountry camping; lodging in nearby communities. Guides and horses available in summer. Visitor centers, interpretive exhibits, nature walks, campfire programs. Map, page 70.

- ## CHANNEL ISLANDS NP
1901 Spinnaker Drive
Ventura, CA 93001
(805) 658-5730

Five islands make up this offshore sanctuary for marine mammals and seabirds. Park islands accessible by boat and small commercial aircraft. Snorkeling, scuba diving, hiking for day visitors. Overnight camping on Anacapa, Santa Barbara, Santa Rosa, San Miguel; permits required; all supplies must be packed in and out. Visitor center and excursion information available in Ventura on mainland; exhibits, navigational charts, audiovisual programs. Whale-watching in Santa Barbara Channel best from late December through March. Map, page 97.

- ## GUADALUPE MOUNTAINS NP
HC 60, Box 400
Salt Flat, TX 79847
(915) 828-3251

Forested mountains slashed by rugged canyons rise from desert lowlands, exposing a limestone fossil reef formed in a shallow sea some 250 million years ago. Panoramic views and 80 miles of trails delight hikers, campers, horseback riders. Fossils and a diversity of plant and animal life lure natural history buffs. Historic sites include ranches and ruins of a Butterfield Overland Mail station. Permits required for overnight backcountry camping. Visitor centers; ranger-guided hikes and evening programs in summer. No lodging, food, or gasoline within park. Fall best time to visit. Map, pages 122-3.

- ## BISCAYNE NP
P.O. Box 1369
Homestead, FL 33090
(305) 230-7275

Subtropical sea, miles of mangrove shoreline, coral reefs, and 45 low-lying islands called keys. Accessible by private boats and concessionaire-run tour boats. Snorkeling, scuba diving in bay and along reefs. Picnicking, fishing, hiking, birding, and interpretive programs available on mainland. Camping only on Elliott and Boca Chita Keys; limited facilities. Insect repellent advised. Some islands closed in nesting season. Map, page 151.

- ## KATMAI NP & PRESERVE
P.O. Box 7
King Salmon, AK 99613
(907) 246-3305

Rugged coastline backed by snow-clad mountains, the desolate Valley of Ten Thousand Smokes, and a forested lake region. Abundant wildlife includes one of the world's largest land carnivores, the Alaskan brown bear, as well as moose, bald eagles, salmon. Access by commercial aircraft and charter flights. Activities include bear-watching, fishing, camping, guided tours, hiking. June to early September best. Insect repellent advised. Backcountry permits recommended. Reservations required for lodgings at Brooks Camp Lodge, Grosvenor Lake Lodge, and Kulik Lodge. Backpacking, canoeing, and guide services available. Map, pages 174-5.